P9-EGB-942

STOKE THE FIRE WITHIN:
A GUIDE TO IGNITING YOUR LIFE

STOKE THE FIRE WITHIN

A GUIDE TO IGNITING YOUR LIFE

By Charlie Adams

Corby Books

NOTRE DAME, INDIANA

STOKE THE FIRE WITHIN:
A GUIDE TO IGNITING YOUR LIFE

Copyright@ 2008 by Charlie Adams

All rights reserved. No part of this book may be used or reproduced in any manner whatsoever without the expressed permission of the publisher.

10 9 8 7 6 5 4 3 2 1

ISBN 978-0-9776458-3-1

Published by Corby Books
A Division of Corby Publishing
P.O. Box 93
Notre Dame, IN 46556
phone: 574.229-1107
fax: 574.698-7600
email: corbybooks1@aol.com

Manufacturer in the United States of America

TABLE OF CONTENTS

This book is dedicated to my loving wife Nancy and our children Jack, Karley, Abby, Rachel, Lindsy and Grace. We are so proud of you all!

Chapter One

RUNNING THE STEPS

The most powerful lessons on peak performance have come to me through the most unlikely of circumstances over the years.

A gruff TV News camera man came into my life one time and hit me right between the eyes with a baseball bat. At least it felt that way. This man was in my life for two hours at the most, and forever changed the way I look at just about everything. I couldn't tell you his name. He probably doesn't remember me from Adam.

It was on a cool October night in Philadelphia in 1991 when this man revealed to me there are two ways we can approach everything we do in life, personally and professionally.

I was a 29-year-old anchor and reporter at WDSU TV in New Orleans. The city's NFL team – the Saints – were off to their best start ever that year. For the better part of their 25-year-old existence they had been known as the 'Aints' because of their futility. Fans became so frustrated that they often wore sacks over their heads during games to hide their identities.

Not this particular year. The Saints were 7-0 and headed to Philadelphia to face the powerful Eagles. WDSU TV management decided to send me to Philadelphia on Thursday to do reports all the way through Sunday. I was to lead off with a live report via satellite to open the 10 pm news that Thursday night. It was to be the most significant night of my broadcasting career. I was leading the late news. Thousands of viewers would be tuned in for the report. I had to come up with something special!

As I flew to Philadelphia that Thursday I decided I would compare the underdog Saints to Rocky Balboa, the famed boxer from the Academy Award winning movie Rocky. I would do my live report that night right next to the Rocky statue at the Philadelphia Art Museum. There's a famous scene in the movie where Rocky runs those steps during training and jumps up and down at the top of them. There is a statue to this day of him holding his gloves up high. Thousands of people have visited it for inspiration while in Philadelphia. I decided that I would refer to the statue behind me as I did my live report back to New Orleans. I was pleased with the idea.

Upon arriving in Philadelphia, I called the camera man I would be working with that night. He worked at the NBC station there and we were hiring him free lance. I asked him to meet me with his Live Truck at the steps of the Art Museum that night around 9. He grunted a confirmation over the phone. He seemed like a no-nonsense kind of guy.

I drove my rental car to the Art Museum and was standing there when the camera man showed up in the Live Truck. As he got out I summed him up to be in his late 50's or early 60's. He had a lot of gray hair and was coming off a shift so I assumed he'd be ready to get this done and head home after a long day. Punch in. Punch out.

Introductions were exchanged and we got down to business. It was a little after 9 and I was going to broadcast live back to New Orleans at 10 sharp.

"What do you want to do?" he asked. I told him my Saints/Rocky comparison.

"I'd like you to take your tripod and set up by that Rocky statue at the top of the steps," I explained. "I'll stand in front of it as I do my live report."

He just looked at me. This went on for twenty seconds. He seemed a bit irritated.

I wondered why he wasn't hustling to set up.

"Is anything wrong?" I finally asked.

"I'm not doing that crap," he said. He didn't say crap either. He used a saucier word.

My jaw dropped a bit because this just wasn't anticipated. Silence reigned for a few seconds. He just looked at me.

"Uh, why not?" I finally queried.

"Because what you want to do is average," he said as he looked me squarely in the eyes. "I didn't come all the way out here after a long day of working to do something average."

There was a long pause because I had never run into this situation before.

"Well, what do you have in mind?" I finally asked. My shoulders were slumped because what I thought was a cool idea was average in his eyes.

"Alright, you want to do this Rocky and the Saints underdog Cinderella angle," he surmised with a gleam in his eyes. "Here's what we're going to do! You can forget me setting up my camera on a tripod. That's basic. I am going to shoot off my shoulder. I am going to lay enough cable so that when they come to you live we can RUN up all the steps just like in the Rocky movie. That's how you're going to do your live report!"

"WHAT?!" I shrieked. "Are you nuts? Did you say run the steps? There must be at least 70 steps. Do you realize you and I both could fall and crack our skulls? Do you realize you could trip as you are running and drop your $50,000 camera?"

"I sure do," he replied with an excited grin. "That's what's going to make it fun!"

My heart started racing as he hustled off to his Live Truck to set up. There were 72 steps leading up to that statue. Neither one of us would be able to look at the ground as we ran because we had to focus on the camera.

He started practicing running the steps side-ways. He had one arm out for balance as he got a feel for how he could run and shoot at the same time. He quickly trained his peripheral vision to pick up the steps. Feeling like I better get my rear in gear, I started practicing running and stepping and talking at the same time. The clock raced. 9:20. 9:40. 9:55. We were minutes away.

9:59 arrived along with the distinguished voice of WDSU TV anchorman Norman Robinson through my earpiece. The newscast back in

New Orleans was opening. Tens of thousands of viewers were tuned in for the lead story. I was so nervous I could hardly see straight. As I looked over to the camera man he simply winked at me. He was loving this. He was alive! He was pushing me. I felt like I was strapped into the the most electrifying roller coaster ride in the world!

"Let's go live via satellite to Charlie Adams in Philadelphia for our top story tonight," said Robinson. As soon as I was on live, I quickly set the stage of the game and the Saints/Rocky connection, and then I blasted up the steps.

Off we went! Step. Step. Step. Step. Step. Flat Area. More Steps. I didn't trip! We briskly zipped up the steps all the way to the top. When we got there I moved quickly to the Rocky statue. The gruff camera man was right with me every step of the way. He wasn't done with his theatrics. At the statue he held the camera high. He lowered it. He moved all around the statue. Everything was a whirlwind!

I introduced a taped piece and leaned over to catch my breath as the viewers back in New Orleans watched the taped interviews. Shortly afterwards, I wrapped up my super sonic live report, and we were done. My heart continued to rat-tat-tat at a jackhammer pace. Exhilaration raced through my body. I walked around that statue feeling like I could fight all of Rocky's opponents at the same time. Well, maybe not Mr. T in his prime. I had done it! I had gone up all those steps yapping all the time!

The gruff camera man didn't say much. He sort of smiled at me. Maybe it was a satisfying smirk. Deep down I think he realized he had made his point to me, like he probably had to many other younger reporters, and younger people. He packed his gear and drove the Live Truck off into the Philadelphia night. There would be other adventures for him tomorrow. He had come into my life at 9 pm and hit me between the eyes with an incredible lesson on how to look at life. By 10:20 he was gone forever.

Like I said, I can't remember his name. I also can't forget the lesson he taught me.

Thursday became Sunday. I covered the game. The Saints won. Afterwards, I flew back to New Orleans on the team plane. As I walked down the aisle to my seat I passed the players. In the past my presence on the plane had been acknowledged with looks of "there's one of those reporter guys, Charlie What's-His-Name."

Not this night.

Many of the players high fived me as I came by them. "Hey, man, that thing you did on the news the other night was awesome," one player said with a big grin.

I responded with a look of, "Huh?"

"That Rocky thing, man," he said,, "where you ran the steps. That had me so fired up I wanted to play the game that night. I couldn't go to sleep. That was cool, man! How did you come up with that idea to run the steps like Rocky, man?"

"Oh, well, you know, I just had to push my camera man to do it," I said, winking to myself.

Upon getting back to New Orleans I was met with dozens of similar reactions. People came up to me on the street for weeks. I found that my performance at work improved. My writing became crisper. I started looking at everything differently. I even started to hear birds chirping.

It was because of a camera man that would not let me settle for simply being solid. I thought I had a special idea of standing next to the statue while doing my report. He thought it was crap. He rattled my cage and led me to do things I had no idea that I had in me.

That was over 17 years ago and not a day goes by that I don't apply the "Running the Steps" principle to something in my life. I'm not even in TV news anymore, and I still approach almost everything with this principle: There's a good, solid way to do a lot of things, which I like to call "the Tripod way." But then, there's also the "Running the Steps" way.

Marriage? There's the tripod way of a good, solid marriage, or you can run the steps by treating every day of marriage like your first date. Remember the butterflies of excitement?

Your faith? Will you look back and say, "Well, I went to church just about every weekend." Or, will you look back and say, "Wow, I really stepped out in faith and grew a ton!"?

Fitness? There's the tripod way of exercising whenever you get around to it, or you can "run the steps" by getting a pedometer, parking far out in parking lots when it's safe, and briskly taking those steps instead of elevators.

Work? You can do a good, solid job and do what's expected of you, or you can be determined to be the best ever at what you do, with a curiosity as to who was a distant second..

We all have the "running the steps" way within us. It was in me. A guy showed up on a dark night and brought it out of me. You've got it in you!

Take a minute and think about your life. Reflect. Pretend there's a gruff camera man looking at you. Where would he not let you settle anymore? Where would he say, "That's average?" Where in your life do you need to get the tripod and throw it away? Where in your life can you "run the steps"?

"If there is no passion in your life, then have you really lived? Find your passion, whatever it may be. Become it, and let it become you and you will find great things happen FOR you, TO you, and BECAUSE of you."

T. Alan Armstrong

Chapter 2

CARE

I was sitting on the couch with my wife Nancy watching a DVD she had rented. The previews of other films were being shown. One preview was of a film that focused on a preacher man from the 1700's or so who had ended up in a time machine and sent to today's world.

Poor Fella. I'll bet he was ready to go right back when he got a glimpse of today's world!

Apparently he had been in today's rip-roaring world for a couple of weeks, so he was somewhat used to cars and planes and microwaves and Brittany Spears and so forth. The preview scene had him sitting in a movie theater for the first time. As the film played, an actor took God's name in vain.

Now, for many people, there are different levels of how they would care about such a statement if they happened to be sitting there like the preacher man.

- *The first level of care would be to turn to whom ever they are with and say, "Umph. Why do they have to have such language in a film? Umph."*

- *The second level of care would be to get up and leave.*
- *The third level of care would be what this preacher man did in the movie. He burst out of his seat and ran up the aisle into the lobby!*
  "You have got to stop that film,"
  he shouted to anyone in hearing distance.
  "They are taking God's name in vain. You must stop it! Don't you understand?!"
  The lady selling popcorn stood dumbfounded.

As that scene played, I turned to my wife and said, "Wow. That man really cares!"

I share this story not to be preachy, but to illustrate a powerful point of Peak Performance. When you care deeply about anything in life like that preacher man cared about God's name being taken in vain in a movie, you have a chance to leave a legacy. When you care to the third level, you can impact generations. You will inspire people. You can bring on powerful change. You can be a part of incredible experiences. That is the level of PASSION!

If everyone in this world cared to the third level, can you imagine what it would be like?

Caring like that can take a piece of your hide, but so what? Stokers don't settle for the first two levels of care. They relish the third level, and so many good things come from that passion.

There's a saying at the University of Notre Dame regarding people in athletics that have spent many years sacrificing for others and caring deeply about what they do and the organization they are a part of. It is said they leave their blood in the bricks.

George Kelly was a successful assistant football coach at Notre Dame for 17 years. He coached under the legendary Ara Parseghian. Kelly coached 13 of his players to the pro level. Later, Kelly moved into administration and continued to care deeply – to the third level – about anything he could do to make Notre Dame better.

I used to see him put a chilled diet cola in head coach Lou Holtz's car just before Holtz left famed Notre Dame Stadium after games. Kelly wasn't too big to do that humble act. When the small civic club I belonged to needed a speaker to come to Honker's Restaurant to deliver a program, Kelly was there. He wasn't too big to come speak in a little room to about 25 people. He cared to the third level all 75 of his years. If you go out to Notre Dame and hack away at the bricks, you'll find the blood of George Kelly in them.

Try to care deeply to the third level no matter what you do.

For much of my broadcasting career I was a sports

anchor on local TV stations. I was often told by management that my job was one of the lowest priorities in the newsroom. It didn't stop me from caring to the third level.

There was a dreary winter night when I went to great lengths to gather all the high school basketball scores for the ticker that streams across the bottom of the screen during the night's sports segment. I finally got them all in just before the 11:00 news. As I delivered the Sports at 11:25, I noticed the ticker never came up. Afterwards, I waited for the behind-the-scenes person responsible for running the ticker. He was headed out the door when I stopped him and asked what happened.

He nonchalantly explained he had forgotten to load the ticker and that it was never activated. He then looked at me and said, "What's the big deal? It's just the ticker."

I begged to differ. "What about the grandmother who stayed up to see how her granddaughter's team did? What about her?"

He looked at me like I must be from another planet and shook his head as he headed off into the snowy night. Unfortunately, he revealed to me there is another level of care: the "I don't care" level. You've noticed there is a lot of that running around out there.

I didn't bring on a heart attack to myself by stressing out over the ticker disappearance, but it was a burr under my butt all the way home. That's from caring deeply – over a Winamac vs Rochester girl's basketball score, for crying out loud!

Caring deeply to the third level can be costly. When you care that deeply, sometimes you don't exercise the greatest control in the world.

Early in my TV News and Sports broadcasting career I was suspended twice by management for pitching mega hissy fits. I had set the bar extremely high for certain shows, and when problems came I blew up and threw tapes against the wall. To be honest, I should have been fired. Other organizations would have shown my volatile rear the back exit door. But I had management that saw that the deep reason for my explosions was that I cared so much about the product and the customers. They realized I wasn't some egomaniac that turned volcanic for selfish reasons. As a result, they suspended me for a day instead of firing me. Management can't tolerate certain things, and if I had kept it up they would have terminated me, but they patiently rode me out because they saw I cared to the third level.

In 1986 I was running the sports department at KBAK TV in Bakersfield, California, when we had an opening for a weekend sports anchor. I led the search for candidates and went through dozens of audition tapes and resumes. Eventually I got to one that really caught my attention. It was of a man named Greg Kerr from the San Diego area. He had last worked in Greenville, N.C. as the main sports anchor. His resume showed that he was out of work and had been for a stretch of time. I wondered why.

As I got to know more about Greg through interviews I realized he was a man who cared deeply about what he did and the people he served – his viewers. He probably cared too much, but that was his nature. That was the fire he had within. It was a fire that nothing could put out. He told me that one night he was in the sports department working hard to put together the 11pm sports report for his station in Greenville, N.C. He had asked the news department to send a photographer over to videotape a few innings of the local minor league baseball game. The photographer came back to the station and flippantly told Greg he hadn't shot the game. He did so in an uncaring manner. This set Greg off the wrong way. Words were exchanged, and they got into a bit of a scrap.

Greg no longer had a job.

Sometimes the fire within you gets you fired.

He openly told me he was in the wrong and regretted what happened. I could see that he had messed up because he simply cared too much. As the interview process went on I came to realize he was a better sportscaster than I was and he was smarter! As Forest River RV plant manager Floyd Miller says: "Hire people smarter and better than you and let them do their job." That's what I did and Greg went to work! That was twenty years ago, and he is still at the station today. He took over for me when I left the station in 1988. His work ethic and commitment and determination to reach excellence have never once waned. He is probably the hardest worker I have ever seen in TV News. He was recently honored with a key to the city of Bakersfield and given Greg Kerr Day honoring all of his work for the community! How about that?

All Peak Performers care deeply. When Tiger Woods spews off choice language after a wayward tee shot, it's because he cares deeply about how he plays the game of golf. I'm not saying he's right to "turn the air blue" with his language when he doesn't hit the ball well, but it stems from him caring to the third level. Tiger cares about his diet, his appearance, his workout routine, his image, his legacy, his family and how he can impact the world – all to the third level. And it shows.

I was in Colorado Springs in June of 2007 leading a "Travels with Charlie" group motivational tour when I saw "care" personified. We were returning to our hotel in a motor coach. As we pulled up I noticed there were about 50 people in the front lobby where the TV was located. It appeared as if they were watching a game on TV.

We walked into the lobby and I quickly realized they weren't watching a ball game on TV. It was a group of Paralympians meeting on the eve of a qualifying event.

I never will forget the expressions on their faces as the meeting leader went over the details of the next day. The expressions were of deep care for what they were doing as athletes.

Their events wouldn't get major press coverage. They probably wouldn't be in *USA Today* that week, but it didn't matter. Their faces bore powerful care. To them, it was the most serious thing in the world. They had question after question for the meeting leader. They wanted to know every detail of the next day.

They cared deeply, to the third level.

I could write sixteen books on how deeply many teachers care about their students as learners and people. One of my passions as a speaker is delivering Teacher/Staff Appreciation programs to remind them of the incredible job they do in an often thankless profession. Teachers don't seek attention for what they do. It's in their deeply caring nature.

A good friend of mine, Rick Carter, told me a story about his wife, Deborah. She'll probably come after me with a baseball bat after revealing this story because deeply caring people don't do things for attention. As Principal of Rochester Middle School in northern Indiana, Deborah works relentlessly to bring excellence to every part of that school. Extremely professional, she cares about what she wears to school each day. When she can, she buys nice clothes. Rick said she had just bought a really nice leather winter coat when a fire blazed through a mobile home park in the school district. It happened over the weekend, and left one particular family with nothing. The mother of the family came to school that Monday morning with the story of the destruction. They had no clothes. It was bitterly cold. The mother was a tall woman. Deborah Carter is tall. Without blinking, Deborah went to her closet in her office and gave the woman her new leather jacket. She started a clothes drive for the family, and went home to see what other clothes she could get for the similarly sized mother.

I was visiting with a friend one time around 8 pm. His wife, an elementary school teacher, came in the den to excuse herself. She had been preparing the lesson plan for the next day for her students. She was going to bed because she was going to get up at 4 to continue working on the lesson plan. That's caring to the third level.

As a speaker, I have "run the gamut" as far as locations and size of audiences. There have been times where 1400 have been in the audience and times where 14 have been on hand. From time to time, I will fill in on a Sunday morning in a small country church. I spoke at St. John United Church of Christ in Wyatt, IN one time when their pastor was on a trip. There couldn't have been more than 30 people in the pews. What stood out to me is how deeply they cared about their service.

When it came time for the Children's Chat, just one little girl came forward. Luci Jordan still delivered the children's message as if she was giving the keynote at a major Church conference. Brian Schlarb was in charge of saying the prayer after the offering. Deeply nervous, he stumbled and stammered and even came to a dead halt. "I'm not very good at this," he said as he stood in front of the congregation. Brian's voice shook as he groped for the right words to say. A good ten seconds went by as everybody patiently waited. He finished. His prayer came from the heart. The whole service continued on with "good ol' country folks" guiding it home. They weren't the staff from a mega Church in the suburbs, but they cared deeply about their church and every service. It showed.

Before I start any job or project or relationship or anything, I ask myself what level of care I am going to approach it with: the first level, second level, or the powerful third one. No one should ever approach any job or marriage or family without taking dead aim at the third level. Can we care about everything to the third level? No. Pouring Count Chocola cereal with a third level of passionate care just seems odd. But for so many other things in life, it's the way to go. Really, it's the only way to go.

What is left out of this calculation, it seems to me, is the business of caring — caring deeply and passionately, really caring — which is a capacity or an emotion that has almost gone out of our lives.
    Roger Angell, author

Chapter 3

A FORMULA FOR SUCCESS: $C + D = E$

Commitment plus Determination leads to or equals Excellence. This is a powerful formula for Peak Performance. I have observed it time and time again in my days as a news and sports broadcast journalist across the nation. I have seen incredible things accomplished by those that put this equation into play. Over the next few chapters I will explain it in depth.

The $C + D = E$ formula was driven home to me on a go kart track next to a putt putt course, of all places. It was February of 2004 and I was in Daytona Beach, Florida covering events leading up to the Daytona 500 race. Tuesday of that week would turn out to be quite a day to remember! It started with my news photographer, Brian Sapp, waking up sick as a dog. He was whiter than rice as he had a case of the flu. Being a team player, and loopy in the head, Brian was determined to gut it out. To give you an idea of how sick he was, when we ate at I.H.O.P. all he had was half a bowl of rice crispies. That's sick! People all over the restaurant kept

23

looking at him like, "Why would a guy come to I.H.O.P. and eat a kiddy box of Rice Crispies!?"

Brian performed "functional, zombie-like work" all day. We worked with our satellite truck operator, Thurman, from the crack of dawn until dark. The three of us then drove our rental car towards Daytona Beach to find a place to eat before getting poor Brian some much needed rest. As we drove along, the cell phone rang. It was Terry Newton of Hoosier Racing Tire. He invited us to "come out and zip around on go karts" on a track they had rented for the evening. It sounded like relaxing fun.

As I pulled up, I noticed that it sounded awfully loud for a place that was supposed to be one of those "Driving Miss Daisy" go kart places. Terry and about 30 of his friends had already started, so I managed my 6'6" frame into one of those low riding go karts and pulled out onto the track. I looked like a preying mantis with my knees sticking up. Despite my contorted, uncomfortable, pretzel-like driving form, I looked forward to puttering around the track and perhaps building up speed once I got the hang of it.

POW!

I got hammered HARD right into the side railing as soon as I tried to merge into the sea of darting go karts. "What in the world?!" I thought. "That guy needs to be careful." I straightened out the go kart and puttered along for a bit.

BAM!

Someone side swiped me right into the railing again! Somewhat exasperated, I got back on track when all of the sudden I got hit from behind and completely spun out! I looked up and there staring me right in the face with a big grin was Tony Stewart! He is one of the top race car drivers in the world. I had no idea he would be there. Amused by spinning me around, he zoomed off. Other go karts came screaming right at me and past me! I quickly realized I was in way over my head. These were all Hoosier Racing Tire employees or professional race car drivers. They were going all out, whooping and hollering along the way! Stewart had been a friend of the Hoosier Racing Tire family for years, and was out there to have fun and race hard!

Our buddy, Thurman the meek Satellite Truck operator, immediately pulled over and got out of his go kart for good. The racing was way too intense for him! He was on his cell phone excitedly calling his buddies to let them know what the heck he had just experienced – for 20 seconds or so before he bailed! I never will forget the sight of flu stricken, pale face Brian. So numb with exhaustion, he just rode around like he was on auto pilot. Go karts knocked him around, but he was in another world of near death and just kept going. I don't think he realized he was getting repeatedly knocked into the railing.

As the racing continued, I learned that I could stay safe in all this intensity by staying on the outside of the lane. They all wanted the inside. I drove around safely for a few laps content to stay in the "survive" mode. Then, the fire within me got stoked! I was tired of being "Grandma go kart driver." I made an instant decision that I was going to the inside lane and staying there!

I committed to it, and I do so with a fiery determination! I swerved to the inside lane, secured position, and held on with ferocity as things got crazy! Darting go karts started diving in at me like fighter planes. They rammed into me, looking for my position. I wouldn't budge. I was committed. I was determined. I even started yelling and probably looked quite stupid doing so, but I had instantly reached a level of excellence as a driver.

Granted, NASCAR and Indy Racing League teams have not beaten down my door to sign me up as a driver, but by being committed and determined I hung with those people for 45 non-stop, crazy minutes of racing. Tony Stewart even came over and struck up a conversation with me after the race. I'm sure he remembers me to this day . . .

I learned something that night. In life, challenges will come at us. It is very important that we don't let them take control. On that night the challenges were diving go karts trying to knock me out of my inside position. Though they kept coming, I never let them take control.

This *Stoke the Fire* principle applies to far more serious things.

A dear friend of mine was a sportscaster named Paul Hartlage. He was burly Minnesota native with a Dick Tracy jaw line and a heart the size of a bear. Paul was the radio voice of the University of Memphis football and basketball teams. In his early 40's he was diagnosed with cancer of the esophagus. It was a death sentence. Though he was not against hope and miracles, he knew he was looking at about a year of life. Cancer of the esophagus means business and many times goes through people like Sherman went through Georgia.

Over that year the cancer would tear him up, but he never let it be in control. You see, he was committed and determined to fulfill his duties as radio play-by-play man of the football and basketball teams. He would not let the cancer dictate totally how he led his life. Sure, it wore him out and caused him to spend a lot of time in treatment, but he spat in its face when it came to affecting his passion for broadcasting games. In some games Paul would lean over, remove his headset, and throw up into a trash can during radio commercial time outs. But he kept going. One time it took him 45 minutes to walk up stairs to the broadcasting booth at Vanderbilt University, but he did it. After the game he got his broadcast partner to carry him to the car and lay him in the back seat. He fell exhausted into sleep for the long drive from Nashville back to Memphis. The cancer took him from 289 pounds to about 120, but he never let it take control. He did his job with excellence through the fall and winter.

In the spring he was just a shell of his former self, but he wasn't done. Part of his duties as the voice of the Tigers was to emcee the annual basketball banquet every year. The cancer had ravaged him and very much wanted him to lie down and accept death. He looked it right in its pond scum face and told it that he wasn't finished with his year. Too weak to walk, Paul was rolled to the podium in a wheelchair where he guided the events of awards night. Then, his job for the year was done. Then, he told the cancer it could take him. He told it. It didn't tell him.

As vicious as it was, he made the cancer of the esophagus bounce off him like those go karts on that February night in Daytona. It probably ticked that cancer off to no end that Paul didn't resign to his fate. He made a commitment to honor his duties as a broadcaster. He did so with fiery determination, and to this day is remembered for the excellence he brought to his position.

Commitment + Determination = Excellence.

A common denominator of my life has been that anything I have been totally committed to is something that I have succeeded in almost every time. Not every time, but a large majority. When I look back at failures, I see a lack of commitment. "Well, if this doesn't work then I always have the other thing that I can do". Stokers don't wishy wash anything that they are going to spend their precious time doing. As they say, if it's not worth doing right, it's not worth doing.

Stokers commit like a Doberman that's latched onto the ankle of a thief. That Doberman is not going to let go. If anything, he will bite harder. Stokers become so committed that the possibility of failure is not even considered. When Scott Skiles took over as coach of the Chicago Bulls he was asked what would happen if things didn't work out. He said to be honest he hadn't even thought about things not working.

A firm commitment means "will" will come into play. Stokers find that they can "will" excellence and success. It is impossible to describe, but it happens.

Years ago I was a young sports anchor at WSBT TV in South Bend. It was Friday night and that meant our team was committed to excellence in coverage of the local high school football games. Being saturated in team spirit, I had picked up a camera to help shoot games so that we could have as many as possible for our customers, the viewers, to see on the show that night. I was at a game between Washington High and Mishawaka High at historic School Field in South Bend. The game was very exciting and close. Back and forth! I kept looking at my watch realizing I needed to get back to the station. It was after 9:30 and the show started around 10:12. I was the host! But I was commited and determined to stay until the outcome of the game was determined. Fans in the stands even started saying, "Charlie, shouldn't you be back at the TV station." That's when you KNOW you've stayed too long!

That's where you "will" things to happen. The game finally ended at 9:40 and I sprinted to the news vehicle. "Excuse me!" I would say as I darted around exiting fans. I jumped into the car and sped back towards the station. Please don't tell anyone, but I was a tad over the speed limit. I knew because the car lifted up into the air as I went over a rising hill.

As I got back to the station I knew I wouldn't have time to park in the back. I roared onto the sidewalk in front of the front door and left the car running in park. I dashed into the building and screamed for anyone to go park the car! As I ran down the hall to an edit suite, co-workers started coming up to me because I was the host and leader of the show. They wanted to know this and that about the show.

"Don't talk to me!" I screamed. "Get the rest of the show together and I will edit this game." I furiously slammed into the edit room suite chair and rewound the tapes. Having no time to play with, I pounded the keys and buttons and I spliced the plays together!

It was 10:10. The show started in two minutes.

Co-workers stood outside the edit room suite with scripts for all of the other games in the show. I finished editing the tape and bounced out of the room. "Give me the scripts! Here, take the tape!"

"Aren't you going to put on makeup and your suit and tie?" one asked.

"No time," I answered tersely.

The opening segment to the show started playing. I warped sped into the studio and ran to the seat next to the anchor, who bore a wide eyed expression as I blasted onto the set! I had time enough to pat my hair down and rub the shine off my forehead, and that was it. The show started. The anchor turned to me and said, "Well! Charlie Adams just roared in here to deliver our Friday Night Football show. Charlie, you are out of breath!"

"I just got back from one of the most exciting games I've ever seen," I said passionately.

Viewers that had tuned in did not see me wearing a blazer and snappy tie. There had been no time to put on them. Instead, I still had the brown sweater I had worn out to the game.

"The folks at home are going to love these high-lights!!"

I roared through the show having not seen a single hilite or gone over a script. It was crazy, but it got done. People on the streets talked about it for weeks. When Stokers grit their teeth and make a commitment, they can "will" their way to achieving their goal.

C + D = E

Commitment has to be the foundation. The course to success may have to be adjusted along the way. Success is not always a straight line, but the bottom line is the iron clad commitment has to be there. It ignites the action and keeps the goal in view.

Determination follows up as the fuel!

"Desire is the key to motivation, but it's determination and commitment to an unrelenting pursuit of your goal — a commitment to excellence — that will enable you to attain the success you seek."

   Mario Andretti

CHAPTER 4

DETERMINATION: THE FUEL FOR THE STOKER

As motivational speaker Pete Walkey says, "Don't be blinded by the simplicity of the statement." Determination is huge for the peak performer. Through it, you can get to the point to where you literally "will" things to happen successfully.

I firmly believe we all have a fire within us. When it gets stoked, look out!

There is a basketball player named Sydney Smallbone. Her youth basketball coach and trainer Rod Creech once told me a story of when Sydney was a couple of years old. She was at the top of the steps at her home when she tumbled down a whole bunch of steps!

Bomp. Bomp. Bomp. Thud. Bomp. Bomp. WHAP!

The family heard it from the other room and knew what had happened. They all came running like crazy with horrified expressions expecting to see baby Sydney squalling at the bottom of the steps. Instead, they rounded the corner to see her screaming at the steps!

Arrrrgh!! Rrrraaaarrrgh! Aaaarrrrgh!

She wasn't crying. Forget crying. She was letting the stairs have it for being there and leading to that unpleasant experience! She was ticked off!

Sydney took that fiery determination and put it into an unparalleled work ethic that led her to a full scholarship to play basketball for the famed Lady Vols basketball program of legendary coach Pat Summit. There are hundreds of girls with more athletic ability than Sydney, but few that can match her for C + D = E. In the summer, Sydney would get up at the crack of dawn to train while others were sleeping. Before games, she would go to another gym and shoot hundreds of shots. Her dream of playing for Tennessee came true.

I was deep into my college experience when I realized, point blank, what I wanted to do as a profession. I happened to walk by the Journalism Building at the University of Mississippi. A sign was posted that read: Tryouts for Student TV News, Weather and Sports. Everything came into focus for me. Sportscasting! That's what my passion had always been. I had never put two and two together to realize I could actually cover sports for a living.

I immediately put C + D = E into effect. Standing at the bottom of those steps, I made an internal commitment that I would bulldoze any barrier in my way. Showing determination, I bounded up those steps and strode confidently into the lobby. "Who do I see about trying out for the Sports position?" I asked to whoever wanted to come out of their office. Two bodies emerged with curiosity. They could tell I meant business. I secured a spot in the tryouts.

I was flat out awful on tryout night. I was so nervous I could hardly swallow. My southern accent made Jeff Foxworthy sound like Prince Charles. The knot on my tie was as big as a grapefruit. Thank goodness most everyone else wanted to anchor News and Weather. Only one other person showed up to try out for Sports. By default I got to anchor the Sports a couple of nights a week on the campus TV station.

As former Indiana University football coach Bill Mallory used to say, I "locked my jaw" and went to work. As famed golf instructor Harvey Penick would say, I "took dead aim" on my goal. I worked as hard as anyone in the Journalism Building, and

I wasn't even majoring in Journalism or Communications. On weekends I would go to the home of the campus TV station engineer and get the keys to the edit suite. I would go back to campus and practice and practice and practice. Many Fraternity students throughout campus would turn on our 6 pm cable newscast to laugh at us and all the mistakes we would make on the live broadcasts. It didn't matter. We kept pressing forward. As an intern at WHBQ TV in Memphis I would cover a college football game all day Saturday. I would then stay at the station until two in the morning editing stories they could run for the next week for the whopping fee of $35 per report.

Three years after standing at the bottom of the steps of the Journalism Building with a spirit of commitment and determination, I was in Los Angeles accepting a Golden Microphone for Broadcasting Excellence at the Universal Sheraton. I was the Sports Director at KBAK TV in Bakersfield.

C + D = E.

One of the most determined people I have ever met is a News Anchor named Cindy Ward. She has been a driving force at WSBT TV in South

Bend for two decades. She is a living example of C + D = E. I worked with her for 16 years and saw first hand her commitment to providing quality local news to her viewers. If a plant was closed, she was fiercely determined to work the phone to get the truth as to why the plant was closing – not just the company line.

Cindy has always been more interested in the quality of the content of the newscast than her own vanity. I wish I had a nickel for every time she has waited until the last few minutes before going to get "spruced up" in the wardrobe and makeup area of the TV station. Her top priority has always been to help produce a top quality newscast. Going to get spiffy looking has always come second.

One time she rushed out of the makeup area to make it to the 5:00 News set on time. It was 4:58. Cindy's long earpiece chord dangled from one ear all the way down to the floor. She hustled down the hall and into the studio. Suddenly, the end of her ear piece chord got stuck in the studio doors. The sudden jerk caused her to lose her balance and she fell hard. She looked like Charlie Brown when Lucy would pick up the football as Charlie tried to kick it! She threw out an arm to break the fall, and broke her wrist in three places!

It was 4:59. What did she do? Go to the E.R. like any sane person, right?

No! She anchored the 5:00 news. Her customers were depending on her. Plus, there was no one else there to anchor. In her eyes, she HAD to anchor. It was her determination that gave her the fuel to gut it out over the next 30 minutes. Then, she went to the doctor. He gave her an earful about waiting so long before coming to get the injury treated. What could she say?

It's a determination thing.

When it comes to determination, Nick Missos provides a tremendous example. I first became aware of him when I read a story on him in the *South Bend Tribune* by Al Lesar. Nick wanted to wrestle in high school, but he had two things going against him. He was legally blind and he was weak. But, he made a commitment to wrestle, and he was determined to make it.

Like so many things in life, it was rough at first. That's why you have to have the commitment to stick it through. It is vital! Nick would be the first to tell you he was pitiful at first. Being legally blind, he was having a hard time seeing his opponents, and he didn't have much strength. The match would start and, woom, he would find himself flat on his back with his legs flailing as his opponent pinned him. This usually happened seconds into the match. That's when the power of short term goals came in. Nick and his coach, Tony Boley, started setting short term goals.

- *Make it a minute before getting pinned.*
- *Make it two minutes before getting pinned.*
- *Make it a whole match without getting pinned.*

I think those are the coolest Short Term Goals I have ever heard of! Too often people set vague goals. Nick was setting realistic short term goals, and slowly but surely the committed, determined young man started reaching them. He never won a match that 9th-grade year, but he didn't quit, and he got to where he was avoiding being pinned. Midway through his 10th-grade year he won a match! He helped his team advance fairly far into the State Tournament. He was a peak performer, getting the most out of his God given abilities.

I shared his story when I delivered the *Stoke the Fire Within* keynote at a Medical Office Manager's Conference. I got this note later from one of the women in attendance:

"I loved the story of the legally blind wrestler and his short term goals. I've been thinking of quitting smoking and I can use your goals example. I am not going to set a goal to quit smoking. Instead, I am going to set a goal not to smoke for one day. Then two days. Then a week. A month, and so on. I think I can meet the long term goal to quit smoking easier using this plan."

I want to give you an opportunity now to write down a short term goal in certain key areas of your life. I know, you're going, "Oh, no, he's going to have me write my goals down now!" Well, it's been written over and over that less than 5% of people have written down their goals, long range or short term. The experts say it's because of fear and having to commit to them, BUT if you are reading this book then you are a Stoker so it shouldn't be an issue. Write those suckers down. A 9th-grade kid wrote them down, and look what it did for him!

Nick has gone through life embracing challenges. Unfortunately, a lot of people go through life with a big chip on their shoulder. They're miffed about this, and mad about that. They have embraced the "victim" mentality and the chip rides right next to their head. That kind of chip is no good; however I do believe Stokers can benefit from certain chips on their shoulders. They are the kind of chips that come when they're told they can't do something, or they're not the right person for the job.

That chip can turn regular unleaded determination into premium unleaded determination.

I started my broadcasting career as a sportscaster. As the years went by management moved me into news and had me anchor the Saturday Morning newscast. That meant I went from saying "there's a long fly ball" to "the homicide victim has been identified as..." When this move happened, I became committed and determined to do everything I could to help the Saturday Morning News reach excellence.

However, not everyone felt I could do such a thing. A management exec pulled me aside one time and said a few people questioned the move of me going into News. I said, "Really? Why?" He said that the perception was I was "just a sports guy" and could embarrass the newsroom by anchoring news. For some reason they felt I would get silly with the news stories.

That ticked me off.

I locked my jaw and became even more determined

to do a top quality job of delivering the news with dignity. It fueled me. I went forward with a mentality of "I'll show them." I ended up anchoring the Saturday Morning News for over four years and got many comments from people that said they enjoyed the credibility of the broadcast.

In that case, I used a particular chip to motivate me. Not a chip about life, but about my ability to anchor news. There's a difference. People don't know the fire that's within YOU. They may think they know, but they really don't. When they question your ability, stoke your fire within and show them what you're made of. Day after day!

When I left TV News to form a full time motivational speaking, training and coaching business, I had many people that believed in me, and many people that looked at me with the oddest expressions. They didn't believe it would last. They were thinking, "This guy was just a sports anchor for small TV stations. Why does he think he can be a motivational speaker?"

There will always be people that either don't "get" you, understand you, or realize the fire within you. They don't really know you. They will want to label you and box you and keep you comfortably fitted into their view of you. They may never really respect you, but Stokers keep going and don't worry about what they think. If anything, they use it as part of the Determination fuel.

My determination as a news anchor and as a motivational speaker has paled in comparison to many of the people I covered out in the field as a news reporter. One of the most powerful stories I ever put together during my WSBT TV News days in South Bend was on a man named Brett Eastburn. I delivered regular inspirational stories called "Making a Difference." I had heard about a fellow born with no arms and no legs who did not consider himself disabled or handicapped at all! I was like, "Really?!" So, I did a story on Brett when he delivered a motivational program to a group of Middle School students. I was blown away by the guy and his incredible attitude on life. I went on to become friends with him and never once saw him mope around. He was always upbeat and always looking on the bright side of things. As I learned more about Brett, I learned he applied the $C + D = E$ formula quite often in his remarkable life.

Years ago he had been a greeter for a large store. Shoppers would come in and he would greet them with a big smile. He liked his job, but he aspired to move up in the company. Brett wanted to move into security. He was committed. He was determined. He just had to convince the boss man. The boss man listened intently in his office as Brett expressed his interest in working security.

"It can't happen, Brett," he said, sympathetically, but matter of factly.

"Why not?" answer Brett.

"You would have to pass a test showing you could deliver a forearm blow in case a shoplifter got rough with you, Brett. I'm sorry, but you don't even have a forearm."

The fire within Brett got stoked. He remembered his wrestling days at John Glenn High School in Walkerton, IN. He had used his incredible upper body strength and leverage to achieve success. He KNEW he could be an excellence security guard. In a flash, he hopped off his motorized wheel chair onto his boss, knocking him to the floor. He contorted his body and dug his stubs into him and held him to the ground. The boss finally wriggled loose, bounced up, straightened his hair and the look of semi shock on his face, and said, "You're hired! You can move into security!"

Brett went on to do an excellent job as he nabbed those dastardly people who who don't like to pay for things in stores. He is now one of the nation's top motivational speakers.

Please don't read this and go to work tomorrow and ask to see your boss and then pin boss to the ground. You will get suspended, fired and arrested all in one swoop!

Please do take the fire that's within the likes of Brett Eastburn, Nick Missos and Sydney Smallbone and know that C + D = E is a Peak Performance formula that works!

I know a very talented author named April Pulley Sayre. She is an award winning author of over 55 natural history books for young people and grownups. 55 books! That's a lot! Yes, but it's a fraction of how many times she has been rejected as an author. She jokingly used to call herself the "Queen of Rejection" because she got so many notes back from publishers not interested in her particular work. She stayed determined and eventually found publishers who recognized her gift for writing.

I love to watch the nature shows on television. To me, there's not much better than a documentary following a tiger around as he goes on the hunt. I was watching one night when the narrator said the tiger succeeded twenty percent of the time at best. That means he fails four out of every five times. But when he succeeds, it's big meal time. When I speak to people in sales I often conclude by saying, "Get out there and fail!" I say that to specifically hit home with the people there that have issues with rejection. I'm not about failure. In fact, I love the line actor Ed Harris says in Apollo 13: "Failure is not an option." It wasn't for them as they were determined to bring the men back safely. In baseball and sales, the success percentage often hovers around three successes for every ten tries. For whatever reason a lot of clients will simply say no. That's just the way it is. It's usually nothing personal. Eventually, there will be those that say yes. You build off of those people and stay determined to keep getting better and better.

However, as much as I believe in Determination, I have to say at times it can be a negative. I harp on the C + D = E formula a lot. There is also the dreaded DD formula. I am not talking about a battery.

I mean Dumb Determination.

Here is an example. I was delivering the *Stoke the Fire Within* keynote to a group of educators in a Midwest state. Early on I could tell they were in festive spirits so I went heavy on humor material. They were laughing at me like I was Robin Williams, Larry the Cable Guy, and Bob Newhart rolled into one. It was side splitting humor! I stayed heavy on humor and it was a great evening! The next week I was in another state addressing a group of educators. I brought out the funny stuff and in return got a smattering of chuckles, if that. They just didn't think I was all that funny.

Being determined, I kept on with my funny stories. Surely they would come to their senses and laugh like the audience from the previous week! The tepid laughter stayed the same. This was an audience that wanted pure motivation and tools for success. They didn't come for the funny stuff. Did I ever change course? No, because I was Dumb Determined. As my dad used to say, I was stubborn as a mule. I kept digging deep with funny stuff, and kept digging a deeper hole. Sixty straight minutes.

Determination is a powerful thing, but every once in awhile you have to watch out for its cousin Dumb Determination.

"The difference between the impossible and the possible lies within a person's determination."

Tommy Lasorda

"The above quote is true, as long as it is not Dumb Determination."

Charlie Adams

Chapter 5

EXCELLENCE: JUST BE IT

In my broadcasting days I interviewed one-on-one such dynamic achievers as Michael Jordan, Tiger Woods, Burt Lancaster, and triathlete Paula Newby-Fraser. It would be easy to write in depth about them, but in this book you will find a great deal of content centered on "folks like you and me." We are people that are committed and determined to reach excellence, but who aren't famous. To be honest, I think we can relate to folks like us better. Plus, you don't have to be famous or a newsmaker to be a Stoker who is the very best at what you do.

The story of Darin Pritchet is an example. Chances are you've never heard of Darin, or will ever hear him on the radio. He's not famous nationally, or regionally, or in his state. It doesn't matter. He seeks excellence in all that he does. Darin hosts a nightly radio talk show known as "Weekday SportsBeat" on News Talk 960 radio in South Bend, IN. I tune in when I can, and am always impressed with the professionalism of the show. One time I was at a retreat center when a corporate businessman came up to me and said, "Charlie, I listen to that Darin Pritchet. I've listened to him for years. I have never heard him say 'Uh' or 'Um' or 'you know' or anything like that. Ever!"

"Really?" I answered, with a surprised look on my face. I had never really thought about it, but surely Darin had an "Uh" in there once or twice! After all, he was on the air 90 minutes a night, 5 nights a week.

I called Darin and asked him about the "Uh" situation. "Well, Charlie," he answered in a humble manner, "I don't believe I have ever said 'uh' on air. When I decided to go into this profession I made a commitment to speak the English language in a very professional manner. I decided that if I ever did have to pause for thought I would do just that – pause for thought. I studied people like Bob Costas and other high achievers that had excellent control of their speech."

Ever since then I have listened to Darin, intently waiting for an "Uh." I'm still waiting.

THAT is excellence! He does it night-in and night-out on a fairly small radio station in northern Indiana. He doesn't set a standard for excellence because he is on a national radio show. He does it because it is the thing to do, regardless of the magnitude of the show. Darin and his highly respected co-host Rick Carter have a large sized, loyal audience in their area because their program is built on consistently being excellent.

Could Darin work for national radio audiences? Absolutely. Does he? No. His wife is from the South Bend area and that's where they want to raise their family.

Just be excellence (this slogan could be a cousin to the Nike slogan . . .) wherever you are. The nationally known people aren't always the best.

The absolute best TV sportscaster I have seen in the last 30 years is not one of the famous network broadcasters. Not Bob Costas or Al Michaels or any of them. The best is a guy named Michael Rubenstein. Being a Mississippi native, I used to watch his nightly sportscast on WLBT in Jackson, Mississippi. It was excellence every night.

It was filled with the absolute latest sports news, investigative sports news, a feature of a local athlete, and crisp, intelligent writing. An honors graduate of Vanderbilt University, the cerebral Rubenstein brought in a huge audience to the station. From what I understood, stations in big markets offered him big bucks to come do the sports there, but he turned them down. He was a Mississippi boy from Booneville who loved his state.

His fire was stoked to produce and anchor sports-casts for WLBT for 16 years, and then a new fire was lit within him. Over a casual lunch of red beans and dreams, as he likes to say, he helped launch the Mississippi Sports Hall of Fame. He has been the executive director of this shrine to greats like Walter Payton, Archie Manning and Jerry Rice. He cares deeply about their legacy. Rubenstein is leaving a legacy. Those things can happen when you care deeply to the third level, like the story of that preacher man in the movie theater lobby.

Stokers don't settle. They don't necessarily have to work unreal hours every day and live unbalanced lives, but they get to where they can't do anything but get better day after day. They relish new challenges. Former Notre Dame football coach Lou Holtz used to say, "If what you did yesterday seems important, you haven't done anything today."

That's a good one. Of course, if you got married yesterday, you'd have a hard time topping that the next day! Stokers simply will not allow themselves to get caught up in the excellent work they constantly produce. They have an intangible that's hard to put a finger on, but basically it's like every time they do something, they're doing it for the first time. Just because they did it great in the past doesn't mean they're guaranteed to do it great the next time. They're confident, don't get me wrong, but they don't take their performance for granted.

A few years ago I had delivered the *Stoke the Fire Within* keynote at the five year anniversary of a company. Ironically, a few days later another company brought me in to deliver an inspirational and entertainment program at their twenty-year anniversary.

As I traveled to the second one I was focused and "on the balls of my feet" as I prepared for the show. I then said to myself, "Charlie, hey, you just did this program a few days ago. You know how to do it. You'll do fine." But it didn't matter. Even though I had done the program recently, I still had to do it again. I did not take it lightly and would not let myself get into a comfort zone. Confident zone? Yes. Comfort zone. No.

One of my best suggestions for "being excellence" is to study those who exude everything that is excellence. As a Peak Performance expert (don't ask my for an I.D. card proving I am such a thing . . .) I study high achievers for a living. I have gained a great deal of insight by the programs I watch on television. People say television is awful and bad for us. Yes, it can be with so much garbage on it, but there is a tremendous amount of quality programming if you look for it. When I flip around at night I am looking for biography shows and interview shows. I want shows that probe into what got high achievers to where they wanted to be in life. I am often startled by their failures in life, and then inspired by their perseverance. The night before writing this I watched a biography of comedian and actor Steve Martin. He said he was born with no noticeable gifts. The gist was that he worked his tail off to accomplish the things he has done in his career. I recently watched a biography show on songwriter Paul Simon. He made the comment that even though his father worked a lot and wasn't at home a lot, a comment he made impacted Paul's life significantly. He was in his room singing when his father happened to hear him and walked in. He sincerely told his son that he was very good at it. That comment made a lasting impact. As a parent, that show improved me.

I do not watch prime time television on the networks. Period. It's great if you do, but try to keep it to appointment viewing of no more than one or two a week. People that plop down and watch prime time network television for several hours before bed are hurting their Stoker possibilities in life. Instead, I have satellite, and I go to the Biography Channel and channels of that nature. There is great wisdom on many of them.

The only drawback is that they focus on famous Peak Performers that are household names. They should look into doing a one hour special on a young lady named Vanessa Pruzinsky that I once had the honor of covering as a broadcast journalist. She wasn't known by millions, but what she accomplished certainly trumped many of the better-known high achievers. I covered Notre Dame athletics for sixteen years. The main reason I came to WSBT TV in South Bend in 1988 was that I wanted to cover true student-athletes that sought excellence in everything that they did. I found no shortage of that in covering Notre Dame athletes. When I am speaking to audiences, people often ask me who the most impressive athlete I have covered is. Without hesitation I say Vanessa Pruzinsky. They look at me like, "Who's that?"

Vanessa carried a perfect 4.0 grade point average her entire time at Notre Dame in CHEMICAL ENGINEERING! How hard is that? She was only the third person in the University's history to do that, and the first female ever. At the same time she was also a starter on the powerhouse soccer team. Vanessa was the Rookie of the Year in the Big East Conference in 1999. She was a key player on a team that was consistently ranked in the top five in the nation, and that has won two national championships in the past decade.

She achieved excellence as a student and as an athlete. Vanessa was committed and determined. She had one brutally tough class that led her to tears. The librarian would often have to wake her up at two in the morning so that she could go back to her room for some sleep. As an athlete she had to have ankle surgery one season, but came back to lead a defense that allowed just five goals in one 19-game stretch.

She was excellence. Not excellent, excellence. It was her state of being. She was as close to perfection as any high achiever I ever covered in my broadcasting career.

Vanessa's perfect grade point average in a brutally challenging major is an inspiration because it is up there in the "perfect" range. While she was able to persevere, that kind of pace can take its toll on many of us. As Stokers, we have to be careful that we cut ourselves a break from time to time. I'm not talking about settling, but about understanding that seeking perfection can be damaging. As someone who has strived for Peak Performance, I have dealt with the curse of setting the bar high: No matter how well you do at something, you tend to harp on the one area where you came up a little short. It's that "perfectionist thing."

Then I read a quote by Dr. Harriet Braiker: "Striving for excellence motivates you; striving for perfection is demoralizing."

She's on the mark there, I believe. Striving for perfection is noble and this world would be in a whole lot better shape if everyone was in tune with that, but striving for perfection can demoralize you. Seeking excellence, however, is motivating. I truly believe it can be a state of being. Stokers strive for excellence as a habit and way of life. They care deeply, as I wrote about earlier, and take it hard when things go wrong, but they keep moving on because excellence is their way of life. Be excellence.

"Excellence is the gradual result of always trying to do better."
    Coach Pat Riley

CHAPTER 6

SEPARATING YOURSELF

In interviewing over 1500 high achievers in my broadcasting career, I found a common denominator in Peak Performance. It is the ability to come up with an original way to separate yourself. It is something YOU come up with from the fire within. This particular fire is not the one of determination or intensity, but of creativity and innovation. It's an exciting fire that is different from the intense fire.

It's not as basic as separating yourself by "working a lot of extra hours." It goes beyond that. It is the revelation that you have come up with a way to separate yourself from other Stokers. It requires creative thinking and digging deep. It's down there in your fire. It's unique to you and what you do. You just have to find it. I have shared this concept in *Stoke the Fire Within* customer service seminars for corporate audiences.

To begin with the humorous side of this point, I must say that I once "separated myself" from other speakers when I delivered a talk to a group of college students about the fire within us. Well, I had a different kind of fire within me that particular night! A friend of mine from my broadcasting days had asked me to talk to his college students about building a speech. Tim Ceravolo had left broadcasting to teach at Bethel College in Mishawaka, IN. He asked me specifically to speak on how to construct a speech, not to ramble on about where all I had given talks and what a "big shot" I deemed myself to be.

To set the stage of this infamous moment, I must take you back a few hours on that regretful day. I had stopped by an event at a store that sold cookies and all that good stuff. I plowed through about three rich macadamia nut cookies. My system said, "Whoa, big man. What are you sending down here? That's not Grape Nuts cereal. Give us a break!"

I went on to speak to Tim's class. The Bible makes it clear that God prefers the humble person to the prideful one. I usually get that repeated point, but that night I got off the straight and narrow humility path. I opened the talk by sharing how to build a speech or motivational message. The students paid great attention and nodded often at the wisdom great speaker Charlie was sharing. Then, I got off track, so to speak. I puffed my chest out and started carrying on like deputy Barney Fife on the Andy

Griffith show. Barney would be prone from time to time to strut his stuff, when he really didn't have the reason to!

"This past year I've had the chance to speak in Dallas, Birmingham, Indianapolis and many other places," I said as if I rivaled Zig Ziglar and Tony Robbins on the motivational speaking circuit. At that stage of my speaking career, many of my engagements came because my friend and fellow speaker Craig Tornquist was booked solid and he had referred those engagements to me. Did I tell the students that side of the story? Nope. I just kept puffing up myself.

I was about to "separate myself" as a speaker.

As I look back, it's my belief that God listened in patiently for a while hoping that I would get back on the humble track. After a while He said, "Enough of this!" Remember those rich macadamia nut cookies I had eaten earlier in the night? They started rumbling and all of the sudden, shall we say, I broke audible wind.

"Wrrrrroonk!"

It came out of nowhere. God means business sometimes, and He has a sense of humor. He utilized both to make a point to me. I couldn't believe it. As my dad used to say in the Deep South, I had fired off a "scobie" right in front of that class! Me! The professional speaker. A member of the National Speakers Association for crying out loud!

If I write anything in this book about Stokers being calm under pressure, ignore it. I turned eight shades of red and stumbled all over myself for about thirty seconds. I lost my point and stammered all over the place. The students up front just looked at me. Thank goodness it was a group of Christian College students! They were so polite that they acted as if nothing had happened. I'm sure they were thinking, "This man is telling us how to build a speech. Does he mean a speech should include a segment where we pass gas in front of the audience?"

I "separated myself" as a speaker that night. They probably won't ever forget me! As you read on in this chapter, you'll see that's NOT what I'm talking about when I say Stokers separate themselves!

Four times a year I lead group motivational tours for Edgerton's Travel Group. The trips are known as "Travels with Charlie." I share humor and inspiration along the way. I put together a special DVD for everyone. After the trip, everyone comes to my home for a reunion party. All in all, we have great times! In the spring of 2007 I led a group of 45 on a journey to Charleston and Savannah. There were a couple of examples of "separating yourself" that happened during our time in the beautiful Deep South. Don't worry. I stayed away from macadamia nut cookies!

We arrived in Savannah where Edgerton's Travel had arranged for us to stay at The Mulberry Inn. As we got off the motor coach, an employee was waiting for us with a basket full of shiny apples and a warm, sincere smile. That impressed everyone. That wasn't the only example of "separating yourself" that was to come.

One of the keys to Peak Performance is having quiet time early in the morning. When I am traveling, I like to get up early, throw on a baseball cap, and go to the hotel lobby to sip coffee and have quiet time. It sets the foundation for the day. Sure, I could have coffee in the room, but I prefer to go out in those nice lobbies for the atmosphere. Waking up early is a good thing, I believe, if you want to be a Stoker. The only things that shouldn't ever wake up early are worms. Those darn early birds always get them! Worms should learn to sleep in.

Anyway, back to my point. I woke up early and called down to the front desk to see if they had coffee in the lobby. The friendly voice told me that the coffee would be out a little later. It was barely after 5 am so I started to thank the nice person on the phone and resign myself to making coffee in the room.

"Wait, sir," the voice said excitedly. "We've got a fresh pot of coffee in the office. I'll bring it down to you. I'll be there soon!"

Well, I am not the sharpest tool in the shed right after waking up. My thoughts don't execute as quickly as they do later in the day, but I was alert enough to realize this perky fellow was going to be at my room very soon, and I was standing there in boxers. I frantically grabbed for my jeans and was hopping around on one leg when there was a knock on the door. I almost fell down. I hopped to the door like I was getting ready for a sack race at a company picnic. I was embarrassed that this person would see me looking like a squirrel had made a nest in my hair, and that I had one pants leg on. However, that person never saw me.

I opened the door to find a forearm holding a steaming pot of fresh coffee.

"Here you are, sir! Have a great morning!"

I took the pot, and the forearm disappeared. I never saw the person. That employee knew that

I was probably not dressed appropriately, so he wasn't standing there at the door. He was to the side looking the other way with only his forearm in my view.

I thought that was the coolest thing! When the trip was over I called the organizers at Edgerton's Travel and raved about The Mulberry Inn and how it separated itself in so many ways. There were many more hotels along the river in Savannah, but as far as I was concerned The Mulberry had separated itself to earn my loyalty as a customer.

Separating yourself is a major ingredient for Peak Performance. Remember the story about Kenny McCreary from earlier in this book. He would wheel room service into a room and then set the table for the guests. He would do so in less than 60 seconds because even though they were impressed that their table was getting set he knew better than to go on and on with it. That kind of service shot him up the fast track in management. HE came up with that idea. It was above and beyond what was in the training manual.

I once spoke at a Superintendent's Breakfast where the leader of the Penn-Harris-Madison School Corporation, Jerry Thacker, shared a message on where the school corporation was at that time, and their vision for the future. There was a great deal of wisdom and optimism in his message. The room was filled with adults, including school leaders, the mayor, and community leaders.

There were also three students.

The Superintendent pointed them out and applauded them for their decision to come to the event. It turns out they wanted to be there to learn more about their school and where it was heading. There were over 10,000 students in the school system. Three made the decision to be there. That's nothing against the other kids, because the school system is pure excellence, but these three students separated themselves by doing such a "grown up" thing at their young age. Look out for them down the road!

Everyone knows how hard Indianapolis Colts quarterback Peyton Manning works. He studies film of his opponent for hours on end. Other quarterbacks do that as well, but Manning separates himself in other ways. I once was told that Manning, from time to time, would stay after practice and throw soggy footballs that he had left in a tub of water. People thought, "What is up with that?" Also, before every game, he made sure all the footballs were rubbed down just the way he wanted them. This required staying on the field while everyone else was in the showers.

Lo and behold, he made the Super Bowl and come game day there was a driving rain. It never stopped raining. He made out fine. He was the MVP and his team won. By practicing with soggy footballs, he had separated himself, and didn't have any problems throwing in the rain.

I know a young lady from Plymouth, Indiana named Elaine Hessel. As a young girl she aspired to seek excellence as a basketball player. She worked hard like all Stokers do, but she found a way to separate herself. Elaine walked around the family farm one time looking for a unique way to improve herself. She came up with an astounding way! Elaine noticed the top of the grain bin had uneven levels and edges. She got her father to throw the basketball up on the grain bin every day. Elaine stood at the bottom in a rebounding position. She never knew quite when or where the ball would shoot off the edge. It helped her develop quick reactions and instincts. This unique practice method helped her become one of the best rebounders in school history. She went on to earn a scholarship to Indiana Wesleyan University.

When I was a sportscaster on local TV news stations, it was made clear to me that the sports segment was the lowest priority in the newsroom. That was always uplifting to hear. The logic was that 70 to 80 percent of the viewers were not all that wound up for the sports. They wanted weather, breaking news, hard news, education news, health news and so forth. "When the sports comes on, most viewers don't pay attention," I was told.

I knew that I faced a daunting challenge. I knew I would have to separate myself and the product if I were to gain their attention. I brainstormed. I bounced ideas around. What could I do to bring in that big percentage and at least get them to sample?

Pow! It came to me out of the blue. I developed a concept known as Flash Frame. Normally in TV News that's a bad thing. It's where a video clip is poorly edited and a flash of wrong video pops up. It's disconcerting to the eye. In my case, I made it a positive thing. I started putting in 1/3 of a second of video of someone very famous somewhere in the three minute sportscast. It was always someone universally known, such as Bill Cosby, a former President, Julia Roberts, a local mayor, and so forth. At some points in the sports segment, they would literally flash up. You had to be alert to recognize them.

In the commercial before sports, I talked it up like a carnival announcer outside the big tent. "Be alert for the Flash Frame," I enthusiastically announced. "At some point in sports a well known celebrity or person will pop up! See if you can recognize the person!"

All of the sudden, that 70 to 80 percent that used to phase out suddenly became interested. People like contests. People like games. They were intrigued. They started leaning forward from their living room easy chairs and started staring like a hawk at the sports segment. From that point on I couldn't go anywhere in public without viewers coming up to me on the street to talk about it. "That Flash Frame is great," they would say. "My wife and I love it. When the sports comes on we both stare at the screen. I say, 'Honey, if you are going to blink let me know so we don't blink at the same time. We may miss the Flash Frame!'"

The rest of the sports had to be quality. There had to be substance. There had to be energy and enthusiasm and product knowledge, but the Flash Frame was what separated it from solid to unique.

Separating yourself means advancement. Decision makers take notice. I worked with a TV news reporter named Anne Steffans once at WSBT TV in South Bend. Extremely professional and well prepared, Anne also separated herself from the pack on a regular basis. I remember one time she was doing a story on women who were being assaulted in a dangerous part of town.

Remember my story in Chapter One on running the steps? How that gruff camera man made me do my live report by running up to the Rocky Balboa statue? Anne could have done a humdrum stand-up report from that part of town. Instead, she put on sweats and jeans and taped a scene similar to what some women were going through there. She had a plain clothes officer imitate a hoodlum and chase her across the lawn and throw her to the ground. Bam! She hit the ground hard in the taped segment! Man, was it effective! A Saint Louis TV station learned about her work and gobbled up Anne to work for them faster than you can say Gateway Arch.

Young people sometimes do some of the funniest things to suddenly separate themselves. A business owner told me once he was interviewing candidates for the receptionist position. It meant answer the phone a lot and talking to a lot of people on the phone! Several candidates in their 30's and 40's came in and impressed him with their profession-alism. Towards the end of the day he walked out in the lobby and there was an 18-year-old girl.

"Can I help you," he asked.

"I'm here for the receptionist job," she said confidently.

"Oh, well, the other candidates have a lot more experience than you."

She looked him dead in the eye. "Don't you see? I am a teenage girl. I am ONE with the PHONE!"

She got the job.

One way to separate yourself is develop the ability to remember names. I believe the Dale Carnegie course helped me a lot in that area. I heard of a teacher once who separated himself when it came to remembering the names of the hundreds and hundreds of students he had over the years. He was a gym teacher, I believe. He called every boy "Tiger" and every girl "Sweetie." One time he was coming out of Wal-Mart when two former students who had graduated six year ago started walking towards him. They said his name. He said, "Hey, Tiger. Hey, Sweetie. Good to see you again."

As he walked past them to his car he heard them proudly say to each other, "Coach remembered our names!"

Those are a couple of fun examples of "separating yourself," but seriously it is a common denominator of success among Stokers. Notre Dame Football had a stretch from 1988 to 1993 where they were as good as anyone in America. They won 23 games in a row at one point. A big reason was someone who separated himself from everyone else in America in his chosen profession. Vinny Cerrato was the recruiting coordinator from 1986 to 1991. He was in charge of getting the nation's top high school players to come to Notre Dame. These players had many choices: Southern Cal, Michigan, Ole Miss, Oklahoma, Penn State and on and on. All of the recruiting coordinators of those schools worked 68 hours a day and all that, but Cerrato separated himself. He brainstormed. He stoked his inner creative fire. He came up with an idea that was a piece of work! It was about the time that bulky cell phones were being used. Cerrato would stand on the sidelines next to head coach Lou Holtz during games. He would have a recruit on the phone. He would then listen in as the coach decided on the play. Cerrato would get back on the phone and tell the recruit what play was about to happen. The 18 year old kid felt like the most special person in the world. He would watch on his TV as that play unfolded. Think that kid didn't want to sign right that second with Notre Dame?

Cerrato came up with that because he was a Stoker whose inner fire fanned the flames of creativity.

He has gone on to executive positions with NFL organizations.

In all the years that I ran sports departments at TV stations across America, I can remember only one time where an area Athletic Director specifically asked to come down to my office to meet about the athletes and coaches he or she represented. It was 1991 and I ran the WDSU TV sports department in New Orleans. Yes, back when the gruff camera man made me run the steps to the Rocky statue! Most of our sports coverage at WDSU TV was on the Saints and LSU football. Tulane University didn't get a whole lot of airtime. Well, their new Athletic Director called me up and asked if he could come down to my office to talk about their new vision. I said sure, and he arrived a few days later. He had exciting charts and graphs of all their future plans. He talked passionately about the personalities at Tulane, and the many story ideas on student-athletes. I could tell he was committed and determined to take them to excellence. His fire stoked me!

Because of his meeting, I saw to it that we increased our coverage of Tulane. Who was that man? Dr. Kevin White. He would go onto become the Athletic Director at Notre Dame. He was the only Athletic Director that ever came to me with such a meeting. He separated himself. Stokers do those things and rise through the ranks.

In August of 2007 I delivered a motivational program to all of the educators in the Mt. Morris School Corporation in Michigan. As soon as I finished several men came up to me and brought up that Kevin White had once worked there. I said, "Really?!" They said it was decades ago. He was a young guy, but even back then he told them he would be athletic director at Notre Dame one day. They said, "Kevin, come on. That's NOTRE DAME!" He said it didn't matter. He was going to reach that goal. He did, partly because he separated himself along the way.

One of the finest news reporters I ever worked with was John Patton. John separated himself from every reporter I ever knew. As a result, his work was always excellent. In today's world some people grumble about what some other co-workers do to their work. They point fingers, and flail their arms, and place blame. John never had any part of that nonsense. He took the extra step to make sure his work was always flawless.

John was always assigned the top news story of the day. His story would lead the 6 pm newscast. There was a lot of pressure with that responsibility. John wanted to make sure every part of his story aired correctly. He would work on his story all day long, then he would do something during the newscast that I never saw anyone else ever do. He would discreetly stand in the control room behind the director as the 6 pm newscast aired. The director always has a script to tell him when to bring up the name of an interview subject and so forth, but John would be there as well to make sure everything came up at just the right time in his story. He would always tell the director that he would be there. He wasn't trying to do the director's job. He just wanted to do everything possible to make sure his story aired perfectly.

And it always did.

Other reporters would stand in the newsroom as their story aired. If the name of an interview subject came up a few seconds latc, they would go, "Aw, man. They messed up! Come on!"

John Patton never stood in the newsroom when his stories aired. He was in the control room, guiding his story home. He knew how to close out a work day. His story would finish airing, and he would get his briefcase and go home to his family. He would repeat the same cycle of excellence the next day. And the next . . .

In motivation, we hear a lot about the importance of doing the little things. The little things are actually big things. WSBT TV in South Bend has always had one of the most respected groups of news photographers in the industry. A few years ago the entire staff was working to cover the story of the funeral of a fallen police officer. The photographers got together and made the decision to all wear nice shirts and ties while taping the event. They wanted to do so to show respect. I don't know if those guys even had ties, but they wore them. A little thing? No, a big thing.

When I deliver the *Stoke the Fire Within* keynote at customer service retreats, I often share the story of Ruth Riley. She led the Notre Dame women's basketball team to the 2001 national championship. The 6'5" Riley certainly separated herself by being very tall, but in many classy ways as well. After the title, she became a celebrity. The Notre Dame women's basketball office was getting a stack of fan letters every day for her. I learned later that Ruth, who is extremely humble and gracious, would take those letters home and write thank you notes back that same day. Many times she stayed up until 2 am. How many athletes do you know that would do that?

When I talked about this subject at a Women's Business Leaders event one time, a lady came up to me afterwards raving about the power of hand-written notes. She said she had taken the time to hand write notes for years, and the benefits had been tremendous to her business. It's a classy way of separating yourself, and it shows you care.

Separating yourself is exciting! It's in you. Experts will train you. Educators will teach you. The fire within you can separate you. When you combine a strong work ethic with a commitment and determination to reach excellence ALONG WITH a desire to separate yourself – look out!!

Take some time now to reflect how you or your organization can separate itself. Again, I am not talking about coming into the office two hours earlier and staying two hours later. This is a creativity thing! A bit of the "Think out of the box." innovation. It's exciting because one decision could be a breakthrough like my silly but effective Flash Frame.

Have fun with it!

"Be different, stand out, and work your butt off."
   Reba McIntyre

Chapter 7

A DECISION TO EXCEL, AND "NO MORE!"

When peak performers use the C + D = E formula, they make a firm commitment to succeed. They burrow in with determination. They will not turn back. They are like a tick on an Alabama hound dog. They ain't coming out! The commitment is the foundation for the future.

After making that commitment and lighting that determination within you, it is important to follow up with an act. You must make a decision to excel.

I once reported on a young man named Maurice Stovall who played receiver for Notre Dame. He came out of Pennsylvania as one of the nation's most talented recruits. God had blessed him with size and many physical abilities. He showed flashes of brilliance for his first three seasons at Notre Dame. He caught 61 passes for 1046 yards and seven touchdowns. Many, however, labeled him an underachiever because he wasn't living up to his abilities.

His fire was stoked when the new head coach, Charlie Weis, came in and gave him the business about his weight. Maurice was not a sculpted-body receiver. There were extra pounds that had no business being on him. Weis, who is hefty, looked at him and said, "Maurice, I am going to be the only fat guy around here." That got his attention. The difference between Peak Performers and the rest of the pack is that a lot of people would wince and sulk over such a comment. Maurice did not. It helped him to make a decision to excel right then and there.

He went on a firm exercise regime and got in rip roarin' shape. In his senior season he caught 60 passes for 1023 yards and 11 touchdowns. In one year he basically did more than the three years before! Sure, he benefited from a new offense that threw the ball to him a lot, but the major reason for his success was he made a decision to excel. From that point on, he cut off the things that had held him back before.

That decision enabled him to be a second round draft pick of Tampa Bay in the pro football draft. He remained committed and determined to reach excellence. He became known as the last player to leave the practice field in the pros, and went on to become a starter in his second season. Had he not made that decision to excel before his senior season at Notre Dame it's doubtful he would even be in the professional league.

Maurice made the decision to excel, and then quickly cut off the things that had held him back. He took a hard look at his life and then did something that's very important for Stokers. He said "No More!" to the things that had led to "average" his first three years.

In April of 2006 I was delivering a program with other motivational speakers at the Lansing Civic Center in Michigan. I think I'm tall at 6'6", but when Tim McCormick came out to speak, I felt like a shrimp. He's 6'11." Now, that's tall! As you can imagine, Tim was a basketball player at the college and professional levels. He was never particularly well known by the average fan, but played in the NBA for a number of years for several teams. He battled numerous injuries, but kept coming back!

He shared a story that really hit home with me when it comes to slamming the door on the things that keep you from Peak Performance. Tim recalled a time when he was a reserve for the New York Knicks. Pat Riley was their coach and his job was to turn them from losers into winners. This was at the time when the great Michael Jordan and the Chicago Bulls dominated them and just about everyone else. The Knicks hadn't defeated the Bulls in forever, and during that losing streak Jordan routinely dribbled right through them and dunked on their heads.

As McCormick reveals in his motivational program N.B.A. (Never Be Average), Riley knew that the Knicks had to cut off their wimpy ways. The Knicks were playing the Bulls and had just finished pre game warm-ups when Riley called them into the lockeroom. A video monitor had been set up that showed Jordan dunking easily on them during that long streak of losses to the Bulls. It was rather pitiful.

Riley let them have it! He accused them of being in awe of Jordan and playing like they wanted his autograph. The players just sat there. What could they say? Riley then sternly informed them that things were about to change. He said the first time Jordan came flying towards the basket for an easy dunk he wanted someone to foul him with authority. He didn't want him hurt, but he wanted Jordan to get a message. Riley said he wanted the Knick to lean over Jordan and say two words:

"No more!"

Sure enough, the game started and Jordan started swooping in for his easy Knick dunk. Wham!

He was fouled convincingly and went crashing to the floor. A Knick leaned over him and said, "No more!"

The Knicks surged to a huge lead. Things had changed. They had made a decision to excel, and a part of that was saying "No More" to the things that had kept them in mediocrity and below.

It requires taking a hard look at yourself and being honest about everything that is holding you back from Peak Performance. The fire within in you has to say, "No More!"

Some of us have the strength to say that and slap the floor and the door is closed to whatever has held us back. For some, it's much more complicated. There is a process to go through that often requires the help of others. Saying "No More" can range from serious issues, like alcohol abuse, on down to such things as eating after 9 pm. Saying "No More" doesn't guarantee you the challenge is about to be obliterated. Yours truly is notorious in that area. I can't tell you how many times I have noticed a Men's Fitness magazine in the grocery story that has some guy with abs of steel on the cover. I stand there and say "No More" to sweets and eating junk at night. I don't slap the floor because other grocery shoppers would probably go get the manager, but I mentally say it. Then I go buy frozen chicken breasts and broccoli. Why? Because I read that's what Tiger Woods eats and he is built like a rock. I go home determined to eat nothing but chicken breasts and broccoli. That lasts about two days. My wife gives me an earful about the three bags of frozen chicken breasts in the freezer. Then, we go to her parent's house over the weekend and the frozen Snickers Bars become available. My "No More Sweets" becomes "After This Weekend, No More Sweets!"

But you know what? Even though I haven't had the willpower to go to my original extreme intention, my diet improves every time I do the "No More" routine.

By saying "No More" a process is underway! A spotlight is on the darkness. It's like a director on the set has yelled, "Action!"

It is critical to take action on whatever is holding you back. As my father in Mississippi used to say, "You have to steady get after it." If you want to milk a cow that's out in the field and you stand 30 yards from it with your milking supplies, is the cow going to get milked? No. You have to go to it.

Former Notre Dame football coach Lou Holtz inspired me a great deal regarding my decision to go into full time motivational speaking, training and coaching. In August of 2006 I saw his new autobiography, "Wins, Losses and Lessons." I bought it before getting on a flight from Seattle to Chicago and didn't put it down the entire way. Holtz humbly opened up a great deal about his background and how he got to the top of college football coaching and motivational speaking. There is remarkable content in the book about how anyone, ANYONE, can achieve significant things in their life, especially when they say "No More."

In the book, Holtz shared how he fell for a girl in college. This was a big deal for him because he was so shy growing up that he never went on a date in high school. She unceremoniously dumped him, which sent him into a tailspin of feeling sorry for himself. He allowed her feelings for him to impact how he felt about himself. I was startled to read that he went on a drinking binge that lasted over a week. He slumped over bars all around town and woke up each morning feeling like a ton of bricks had been dumped over his head. But when he got done with his "po' pitiful me" stretch, he realized how idiotic it had been. In his own way he said "No More" to such foolishness and from that day on never had more than an occasional class of wine at dinner and a social drink every once in awhile. He learned then and there to associate alcohol abuse with gloom and despair, and slapped a "No More" in its face! He went on to coach Notre

Dame to the 1988 National Championship and become the first coach to lead five different colleges to bowl games.

Some of us have the fire within to make sudden sweeping stops of the things that are holding us back from Peak Performance. Others have to do it in stages. But the first step is taking the time to reflect and candidly admit to yourself, and others when appropriate, where you need to say, "No more!"

A great motivating force can be to do it for those closest to you. I delivered a motivational program in Mt. Morris, Michigan one time. There were displays set up outside the conference room regarding wise health choices. A brochure caught my eye that had the picture of a man on it. The caption read, "People are depending on you. Your kids need you around for a long time." Their specific point was to take the positive steps for better cholesterol, but that approach of "people are depending on you" is good for many things.

It made me think of when we say "I love you." In most cases we mean it when we say it, but do we show it in everything we do? There is a verse in the Bible that reads: "Dear children, let us stop saying we love each other; let us really show it by our actions." 1 John 3:18. Saying "I love you" also means watching what we eat, how we exercise, what we read, what we do, and what we believe in. It's more than deep emotional feelings. It's action. It's "I love you, so I am going to to say "No More" to the things that could keep me from being my best for you!" Do I love to exercise? No, but a motivating force is that it lengthens life so that I'm around as long as possible for those that need me. Do I love eating sensibly? No. I'd love to eat Cheeze-its all day, but I eat two or three apples a day, whole wheat bread, a decent amount of veggies, and all that healthy stuff so that I can stick around awhile.

Whenever I speak to young people, especially girls, I ask them to picture holding their baby a few years down the road. They smile. I ask them if they will love that baby? They look at me like I'm an idiot. Of course they'll love that baby! Alright then, I say start loving that baby now – years before birth. Make a commitment and have the determination to refuse to settle until you know the person you are marrying is the person for a lasting, solid foundation marriage. By doing that you are saying "I love you" then to your children that won't be born for years. One of the saddest things is to see women marry men who they think they change over years or that will "come around."

Be real, Charlie, you say. It's hard to nail the marriage thing. The marriage success rate is just 50% or so. Well, I'm here to tell you that getting a marriage right can be done. A group of young people in LaPorte, Indiana have shown us that. I was speaking to the Fellowship of Christian Athletes chapter of LaPorte High School in January of 2007. Their director, Dave Krider, told me that in the twenty or more years they had been in existence, they had nine marriages of kids that met within FCA and dated while in FCA. All nine marriages were still going strong. They had a 100% marriage success rate over a quarter of a century. That revealed to me that those kids had starting saying "I love you" to their unborn children by making sure they were marrying someone they would be with the rest of their lives.

I'd love to be in that group, but my first marriage ended in divorce. You too could be in that group of being divorced with kids. Does it mean we don't love our kids as much as someone from a lasting marriage? Of course not, for the most part. Where we don't love them as much is that we didn't make it ironclad certain that the marriage we went into was built on commitment and determination to last.

Take the time to reflect where you can make "I love you" more of an action statement.

I encourage you now to also take the time to reflect on where in your life you need to say, "No More!" in any area. Make it a dramatic moment. Slap the floor. Yell it out. But then, act on it. Some Stokers can firmly say "No More" once and make a lasting, positive change. Others need to slap the floor a few times over a period of time. The bottom line is that when you say "No More" you are making a decision to excel. You have stoked the fire within in you that refuses to put up with crap in your life anymore. You are tired of settling for the things that hold you back.

"What one has to do usually can be done."
  Eleanor Roosevelt

Chapter 8

STOKERS KNOW HOW TO CHILL

When we think of Stokers we sometimes get this image of someone with an intense face and squinted eyes that walks around looking like they're going to pounce on a mountain lion. They're serious! Focused! They have that Peak Performance image!

Good luck trying to stay that way.

The best way to maintain Peak Performance is to know how to chill from time to time. Stokers realize the importance of easing on down, reflecting, and working on their self awareness. Until you truly know who you are and what you stand for, you can be busy as a bee but not fulfill your potential. Part of that comes from resting.

In this book I will share three different stories from tiny St. John United Church of Christ in Wyatt, IN. Some of my greatest inspiration comes from the tiniest of sources! I was speaking there one time when a member named Carroll Shafer showed me their beautiful cemetery behind their church. She reflected on how her late mother, Agnes Schafer, used to cut the grass out there. As she got up in years that used to wear her out! She would always stop and rest and reflect.

When Agnes died in 1951, she asked that her family put a bench over her grave instead of a traditional headstone. I walked out to it one Sunday morning and stood by it. "Rest with me" is engraved on both legs of it. She lays buried next to her husband, Edgar.

Rest with me. It's so important to make sure you take the time to rest. The world will somehow find a way to make it during your chill time. Besides "chilling," it's also important to find ways to poke fun at yourself or your situation no matter how intensely you approach life!

My wife Nancy and I have six children between us, including five girls! When we go out in public, people say, "Catholic, Mormon or Amish?" They are beautiful kids, but at times things can get rather stressful around the house. One thing I try to do when Mt. Charlie is starting to percolate and perhaps spew lava is do a breathing technique. It's simple. Those kinds of things don't have to be complex. I simply breathe in as I count to four. I breathe out as I count to four. It takes four seconds (duh, Charlie) for each step. Darting thoughts are not allowed during that time. I try to picture a peaceful sleeping baby during that time (there is no way I will be invited to speak at a Macho Conference after sharing that insight) and it helps. For awhile.

Some of the most intense people I know are capable of downshifting into the Chill Mode and poking fun at themselves. I once reported on a young man named Mike Edwards. Mike had been born missing a bone in his left leg. The leg didn't grow correctly, leaving amputation as the only option. A dedicated basketball player, Mike held off on the amputation. He would come home from practice and soak his leg in a bucket of ice to handle the brutal pain. Finally, it got to be too much. At 13, he had the amputation and continued to play with an artificial leg.

Mike and his family moved to South Bend. He didn't tell anyone about his leg and earned a spot on the varsity team at John Adams High School based on his basketball skills. He wore sweats all the time to hide his artificial leg. Eventually, he had to take off the sweats. You can imagine how surprised his teammates were! They really didn't know how to act around him. There was a period of awkwardness.

Mike sensed it. Even though he was one of the most intense athletes to ever play at Adams High, he also knew when to loosen things up. As the team rode a bus across town to a scrimmage, Mike took off his artificial leg and held it out the window and waved it at passing cars. His teammates got the biggest charge out of that. Everyone laughed! Then, when they arrived at the opponent's school, Mike put the leg on backwards. With the other school's administrators waiting outside the bus to greet the visitors, Mike walked off with one foot heading forward and the other foot heading backwards. The administrators about hopped out of their pants!

Although Mike is one of the most intense, dedicated people I have ever met, he also knows when to have fun!

I get a big kick every time I think about what happened after I delivered the *Stoke the Fire Within* keynote at a Teacher Appreciation conference near Indianapolis. It was just before the start of the school year. Teachers have intense jobs, but I have found the ones that often last the longest are the ones that can poke fun at themselves. After my talk, a veteran teacher lady sauntered up to me. There were three other teachers there talking to me at the time. They kiddingly rolled their eyes at me as she approached. It was like they were saying, "Get ready for anything!" This teacher was rather stout, shall we say. She looked at me confidently and said, "I'm a piece of work!"

"You don't say?" I replied.

"I'm 67-years-old, " she said. "I've been teaching forever, and I still love it. When I don't, I'll stop teaching. I'm excited about the challenge of another school year. I'm glad to be back in the school building."

There was a pause.

"The only thing I don't like about coming back to teach at the end of summer," she said as she looked down the hall, "is that I have to start wearing my brassiere again!"

We all howled. She smiled, raised an arm, and sauntered towards her classroom!

Successful, but volatile, basketball coach Bob Knight has even shown the ability to poke fun at himself. Many people remember his 1985 infamous chair-throwing incident when his Indiana Hoosiers were in a heated game against bitter rival Purdue. Knight had just received a technical when he hauled off and bounced a chair across the court. The shenanigan was replayed on TV all around the world and followed him for years.

A friend of mine told me of a sales conference he

was attending years ago. The event was about to wrap up when all of the sudden the doors burst open and a chair came flying into the room. It bounced past everyone and surprised the heck out of them. That wasn't the end of the surprises. Bob Knight himself came charging into the room behind the chair! Every one just about fell off their own chairs! Knight went on to deliver a rip-roaring motivational talk. It turns out he was friends with the owner of the company and agreed to speak at the end of their conference.

Knight was able to take one of him more infamous moments – and he's had a few – and make fun of it. As the years went by he even started "claiming" that when he threw the chair during the game he was only trying to get it to a little old lady who didn't have a place to sit (!).

Stokers that go around all the time with that intense "grrrrrrrrrr" approach usually see the fire within them snuff out at some point. Taking chill pills periodically and going with the flow helps a great deal.

I was getting ready to deliver the *Stoke the Fire Within* keynote to hundreds of students in Reese, Michigan one time. My wife had insisted I wear a medium blue long sleeve shirt since "it went with my eyes so well." My wife and I have one of those marriages where I don't try to run her life, and I don't try to run my life, so I ended up wearing the shirt. The problem was I forgot my undershirt. My body gets excited before keynotes, so a few minutes before walking out I noticed that there were HUGE arm pit circles! Aghh! There was nothing I could do.

As they introduced me I said to myself, "You are about to become T Rex man." I went out there and for 60 minutes kept the upper parts of my arm tight to my sides of my chest, and made gestures with my forearms only. I looked like a T Rex. You know how they have those tiny arms for their big bodies?! I'm sure those students were thinking, "My, what strange arm movements that man makes."

Ah, what can you do in times like that? Stress out and implode, or go with the flow?

A state association of postmasters brought me in one time to speak an entire hour strictly on Attitude to open their conference. I prepared the program. I don't really use notes when I speak, but in this case I jotted down the order I wanted to go in the talk. I had written "one word" reminders on the sheet to make sure I got in all my points. Before the session began I laid my notes up on the podium. A few people went before me to make announcements. When it came time for me to speak I arrived at the podium to find my notes missing! Argh! One of the other presenters had accidentally swooped them up when they left.

I was looking at 60 minutes of speaking strictly on Attitude with no notes whatsoever. This was fairly early in my speaking career, so it was a cause for crisis. I could have stumbled and wigged out, but instead started talking to myself as I started my Talk. I said to myself, "Okay, big boy, let's see what you've got! You've got a whole hour to speak with no notes! Woo wee! You are up a creek without a paddle! I would hate to be you right now!" That was a really odd thought, since I was me, but I was making fun of myself in my head! I ended up being more energetic, and got some points out of order, but delivered the talk and they got a big kick out of it.

Eileen Shue is one of the top H.R. managers in the nation. I was talking to her one time when she told me she loved to be around people with H.F.Q. I wondered what that was?! "High Fun Quotient," she said with a smile!

How we respond to the challenges of life has a great deal to do with our ability to perform at high levels. Sudden curve balls come screaming at us and knock us silly. There are always unexpected surprises! Back in the late 1980's I was a sports anchor at KBAK TV in Bakersfield, CA. It was the football season. For some unknown dumb reason I predicated a local powerhouse would lose in the playoffs. Early in the week I said the Garces Rams would fall that coming Friday night. I even said they would be "crushed." What purpose that served, I have no idea. Wisdom and Charlie have not always gone hand in hand.

Their fans quickly called me in the Sports office and let me know that I was going to pay a price that Friday night. They were good natured about it, sort of, but I could tell they meant business! Friday night arrived and I roamed the sidelines reporting the game. It was a rainy, yucky early November night. Mud puddles were all over the field and around it. Many fans had brought homemade signs forecasting my doom once the game was over. Sure enough, Garces won the game. Seconds after it was over several men rushed me and grabbed me! "It's time for you to pay, Charlie! You are going in the mud!"

Ever the showman, I pleaded with them to stop until the KBAK TV camera man Dan Tudor could come over to video tape it! They obliged. Dan arrived, and the process began.

"One, two, three," they yelled in unison as they swayed me back and forth to build momentum for the Great Mud Splash. They released me like they were lumberjacks throwing a log on a pile. Bam! I hit the mud with a mighty splotch! Mud went everywhere. The breath was knocked out of me! They cackled with great delight! The fans in the stands howled with satisfaction. I just lay there in the mud in all my glory.

It was 10 pm. I was to host the Friday Night Football show at 11 pm. I could have stressed out about all the mud caked in my hair, ears and all over my clothes. There was no time to go back to the station and shower and change clothes and so forth. The live broadcast was coming up. I decided to have fun with it! I didn't wipe a bit of mud from my face or clothes. I went on the air that night looking like Pigpen from the Peanuts and Charlie Brown comic strips. The floor crew on the set got the biggest kick out of it. The viewers loved it. I heard about it on the street for weeks.

I had responded to a stressful situation by turning it into a lot of fun. I could have wigged out with, "Oh, no. I've got to change clothes. I'm hosting a show! How could they do this to me! I don't look professional! Ohhhhhh!" Instead, I turned it into pure fun!

21st century life "piles it on us." Added job duties. Budget challenges. Never ending change. You know the drill. For years I have looked for ways to counter the stresses with opportunistic humor. It kept me sane for over two decades in the high pressure world of local TV news.

One time I was part of a crew rumbling back from West Lafayette, IN in the TV station satellite truck. The truck was adorned with all sorts of gaudy logos such as "Live Satellite News" and "Your Source for Breaking News!" We had to stop along the way back to uplink a story back to the station in time for the late news. It was to be a fairly quick stop. We simply needed a parking lot to pull into so the engineer could raise the satellite dish and we could feed the story back to the station.

It had been a brutal 14-hour work day after a whole week of work. I was exhausted. We rumbled through Delphi, IN and came upon a Dairy Queen. Wilson Johnson, the satellite truck operator, pulled the truck into the DQ lot and began the process of raising the dish and feeding the story back to the station. I wearily stumbled out of the truck and stood by it as he did his job.

I noticed a "good ol' boy" walking across the parking lot to go eat at the DQ. I can poke fun at this fellow because I grew up as a "good ol' boy" in Oxford, MS! This fellow, decked in overalls and a repair shop baseball cap, noticed our truck and veered over towards us.

A practical joke immediately came to me. How? I don't know. I suppose I had developed the "rascal" in me over the years as a stress resistance measure! I straightened up and looked very professional and concerned as the fellow walked up to the truck.

"What ya'll doing with your big news truck here in Delphi?" he asked as he gazed at all the gadgets on the truck.

"You haven't heard?" I answered, seeming somewhat surprised.

"Heard whut?"

"Aliens have taken over that Dairy Queen," I said, with my most professional news reporter look.

"WHUT?!"

We both stared in the Dairy Queen. Things looked normal and there were no green people with big ears. He looked at me with an expression of "I don't see no aliens."

"The aliens have taken over the bodies of the workers," I replied, as if I had studied their ways for years and written about them in *National Geographic*. "They are sucking brain waves and energy from the customers and sending that back to their home planet."

"Nawwwwwww!?" he answered as he whipped his neck back and forth between me and the DQ.

"Yes," I countered. "That's why we are here with the satellite truck. We are broadcasting this to CNN. This is major international news."

Our satellite truck operator Wilson had get behind the truck because the giggles were getting to him.

The good ol' boy did his best to process all that had body slammed him. What began as a simple trip to get a medium-sized Blizzard had mushroomed into the potential destruction of many brain waves. He didn't know how to react.

I rubbed my chin and looked very bureaucratic. The longest time seemed to go by. He kept looking back and forth between DQ and our truck. Finally, he spoke.

"Well, hell, I'm going somewhere else to eat!!"

He spun around and off he went into the Delphi night. We left ten minutes later. I never saw the poor guy again. I must admit, I did get to feeling guilty on the ride back home. I also got concerned. What if he went and got his buddies and came back with baseball bats and charged into the DQ. "You aliens better quit taking Delphi brainwaves!" Whack! Whack! I also worried that he ended up in the institution after repeating the story to city officials all over Delphi.

"I'm telling you there WAS a TV truck here to report on aliens. I SAW the truck!"

"I'm sure there was a truck, Jimmy Ray Bob. Now, you come with us and we are going to take you to a nice facility in Indianapolis where you can say all you want about the aliens and the brainwaves."

I must say that I have been in "Jimmy Ray Bob's" position many times. I have had co-workers plan and execute remarkable practical jokes on me. I have been "had" hook, line and sinker as the victim, and laughed about it right along with them.

Stokers try so hard that often the reaction they get to their work disappoints them. I've had times where I worked extra hard for weeks on a special report on the News. The segment aired, and I would get back to the office and hear the phone ringing. I would pick it up anticipating glowing words of praise from an appreciative viewer whose life had been impacted forever by my report on the News!

Instead, I would get this:

"Hey, news man. Your tie was a little crooked on the news tonight."

I just had to chuckle and shake my head and try to laugh about what he took from the news.

As a motivational speaker, I set out to enhance or change lives. I believe passionately in the messages I share because they are fueled by the remarkable people I had the privilege to cover over the years. People do come up after programs and share how the message specifically impacted them, but there are also times where you just have to wonder . . .

Davenport University had asked me to deliver the keynote at their High Honors Graduation ceremony one year. That would be a grand challenge, because it wasn't just the overall graduates. These were the super-motivated students who carried near perfect grade point averages! I prepared a rip-roaring Change the World keynote and was raring to go!

The address would be at a Friday morning breakfast. The overall University commencement would be that night, so it was to be "a day of it" for all the parents and loved ones coming to the area. The weekend happened to be the time of the annual Blair Hills neighborhood Garage Sale where we lived. It was always a big deal that got my wife worked up.

I got up early that Friday morning and put on my dark corporate power suit and headed to my car.

"Where are you going?" my wife Nancy asked.

"You know where I am going." I answered. "To speak at the High Honors breakfast."

"You're not going yet," she said with an intimidating glare. "You've got to help put the Garage Sale things out in the driveway. Get cracking, big man."

I threw my arms up. "Zig Ziglar wouldn't tolerate this just before a talk," I yelled.

"You start getting Zig's keynote fee and I'll hire someone," she said.

I took off my power suit and started hauling couches, baby cribs, and a zillion Barbie Dolls to the garage. We have five girls between us so we have over 23 million Barbie dolls. I put my suit back on and drove furiously to my engagement.

There, I shared the timely story of how earlier in the morning my wife had me setting up for the big Blair Hills garage sale in our neighborhood. The audience chuckled, and I went on with my "Rah Rah Woo Woo" talk.

I went back home that morning and parked down the street. Many little old ladies and their little old lady friends were darting in and out of garages. I walked confidently into our garage knowing that I had impacted generations with my Abe Lincoln-like address.

My wife saw me coming and said, "How was your talk? Good. Glad it went well. Now, sit down at the money box table and run that."

"Can't I change out of my suit?"

"No time, big man."

I shrugged my shoulders and sat down behind the rickety cardboard table deep in our garage. Within minutes several little old ladies started bartering with me over the price of Barbie's. We had those priced three for a dollar and they wanted three for fifty cents.

"No, absolutely not," I answered. I was moody because earlier in the evening I had been a life-altering motivational speaker and now I was running the change box at the Garage Sale! Show me video of Zig ever doing that!

They sneered at me and left to barter someone else down on Barbie's.

I then noticed several other little old ladies staring at me from across the garage. I could tell they recognized me from all my TV news days. They had no idea this was my house. I just knew this is what they were thinking: "That poor Charlie Adams. We heard he left TV news to go into speaking. It must not have worked out. Now the poor man is working garage sales to pick up a few bucks...."
I continued to sit there in all my non-glory when I looked up and saw a somewhat recognizable face. I knew I had seen the man from somewhere. I just couldn't remember where!

"Do I know you?" I asked.

"Well, sort of," he said. "My wife and I were at the High Honors breakfast this morning. Our girl graduates tonight. We were at your talk."

"Ohhhh," I said. Desperate to boost my self esteem, I started fishing for compliments. "Well, what did you think of my talk? How did it impact you? What did you take away from it? What will you put into action? What did you get from it?"

The man looked at me with a bemused expression. He shrugged his shoulders and looked to his wife for help. She just looked back. He stared at me for a moment.

"What did I take from your talk," he finally said. "Well, I guess I learned there was a Garage Sale in the area."

!!!!

That about did me in right there! I just rolled my eyes and laughed to myself. What can you do! I was manning the change box at a Garage Sale and my talk served to inform people of area Garage Sales!

Stokers know how to smile and laugh in life and take the opportunity to have a little fun and even be a rascal from time to time! Like Marty Harrell. I got to know Marty at men's church retreats over the years. He would lead the singing. Marty always had a smile on his face and a lot of love in his heart. He faced serious health challenges in his life, but they never stopped him from getting the most out of every day.

Like the day he wheeled his car around the drive

through at a fast food restaurant in Logansport, Indiana. For the first time he noticed a small sign that indicated Braille Menus were available upon request. Bingo! An opportunity for some fun!

Marty reached over, put on his sunglasses, and got the Steve Wonder head movement down pat. He had the slight head wobble down pat when a young lady's voice came through the speaker asking if she could take his order.

"Yes, but first could you bring out a Braille menu?" Marty asked.

The young manager girl became excited. Not many people made that request. She said she'd be right there. She came darting out with the Braille menu and went right to the passenger's window. Except there was no passenger there or anywhere. This confused her. This had not been covered in manager training. She looked over at Marty and he had his hand out the other way waiting for a menu.

But he was the driver!

She jumped back like a deer spooked by a hunter, and then . . . gave him the menu! Marty rubbed his fingers over it as she scampered back to her post and head set. The poor girl had the look of someone "slightly rattled." Marty ordered number five and she stammered out how much it cost.

Five dollars and nineteen cents.

Then came the time to move the car forward.

In one of the classic moments in the history of the world, Marty reached his left arm out as far as he could and ran his fingertips along the bricks on the building as he started puttering forward! The poor manager girl about fell backwards. With his head tilted back and bobbing ever so slightly, Marty goosed the accelerator and then hit the brakes. Vroom. Errrtt! Vroom. Errrtt! The car erratically moved forward as Marty's hand went from bricks to shrubs as he felt for the next order window.

At this point there were at least three heads sticking out of the order window. Based on the anguished look of the young manager girl, six to ten years of her life had been shaved off from the sudden stress.

Marty got to the payment window and reached for his wallet. He knew he had a 20 and a 5 in it. "Five dollars and nineteen cents, huh?" he asked. "Okay. Would you please tell me which one is the 20 and which one is the 5?" He held them both out pitifully. The manager girl sputtered out which one was which, and he gestured for her to take the right one.

At this point, everyone in the restaurant that was

ordering dine-in had forgotten about their own orders and started staring awestruck at the drive-in window. Marty just continued to bob his head, whistle and hum. Life was good. Food was on its way.

Change was made for the 20 and Marty stuffed it back in his billfold. He then reached that long left arm of his and made contact with the friendly bricks again. His car did the herky jerky advancement a few feet to the pick up window, where a new world record was being set of most heads sticking out at the same time. Marty stared in the general direction of the window and made pleasant small talk. The scary thing about our society is that at no point did anyone stop him. Everyone simply wore a "deer in the headlights" expression as they tried to process what was happening. My theory on that is that's what fast food has done to America. As a nation, we no longer stop blind people from driving.

Marty had his food. He thanked everyone, leaned back, and guided his car out towards traffic. Everyone in the restaurant gawked as he merged into traffic. Astonished looks of horror reflected from his rear view mirror as he purposefully almost hit a car as he merged into traffic. He disappeared into the Logansport day.

A few weeks went by and Marty's hunger led him back to the fast food drive through. He had forgotten all about the "fun" he'd had the last time there. You can imagine his surprise when he pulled up to pay for his order and saw that young manager girl there. It's debatable as to who had a more startled look – him or her! All Marty knew was that the young girl looked terribly confused and desperately needed an answer. With his sunglasses in his glove compartment, he looked up at her and pointed at his eyes and said:

"Praise the Lord. It's a miracle!!!"

Vroom. Off he went!

Every once in awhile in life, you just need to be a rascal.

"Humor is a great thing, a saving thing. The moment it crops up, all our irritations and resentments slip away, and a sunny spirit takes their place."
   Mark Twain

CHAPTER 9

"CHARLIE'S GUIDE TO OODS & ATTITOOOODS"

(My daughter Abby came up with the title to this chapter)

I love listening to speakers. They don't have to roam the floor with a wireless microphone to impress me. Many of the best stand right behind the podium. It's their wisdom and life experiences that I look for.

I had the opportunity once to hear a lady named Sandra Herron from Crystal Cathedral share her life story at Evangel Heights United Methodist Church. Sandra moved just in front of the podium and chose not to bounce all over the room. She shared her many challenges and how various health issues had caused her to "explode" many times. Sandra recalled the time she was in a hospital room for weeks on end. She had no strength. All she could do was lie there. She could barely even lift her arms. Bumps on pickles could do more than she could do. As she lay there, she thought of what she could do to make a difference. She came up with an idea.

Every time a nurse or a worker would come into her room, she would give them a radiant smile. She would hold it. Once they had finished their duties, she would mouth "Thank you" to them – no matter how trivial their task had been. It wasn't long before nurses and other workers started coming to her room for their break time. They wanted to be somewhere warm and loving.

Sandra then said something that has stayed with me ever since: "You can celebrate life or suffer it, and it has absolutely nothing to do with your circumstances."

That's powerful.

It made me think of the saying, "A happy person is not someone with a certain set of circumstances, but with a certain set of attitudes."

Stokers celebrate every day no matter what. They are gloriously aware of what an incredible blessing each day is to them. They don't have to hear the story of a tragedy and the inevitable comment of "this shows us to live our fullest every day because we never know when it's time." Stokers already get that!

I have reported on dozens and dozens of games at famed Notre Dame Stadium. I have always made it a practice to stand near the tunnel after the game ends. I can always count on seeing kids that hang over the railing to get a close view of the Fightin' Irish football players as they walk into the tunnel to go to their locker room. The players are dirty, sweaty and "dog tired" as they walk into the tunnel, but they always have the energy to take off sweat bands, head bands and waist towels so they can toss them up to the clambering hands. Whenever a kid actually catches the treasure of a grass stained wrist band, the expression on their face shows enough energy to light the Stadium for hours. The kid holds the sweat band and stares at with a look of "I've got it!!"

That's how Stokers look at every day. "They've got it!" They know they have the remarkable gift of another day, no matter what challenges exist in it. They understand what an incredible blessing it is and they want to hold it as tightly as a kid holding a grimy sweat band.

One of the most remarkable people I ever met in my TV News days was a lady named Rill Mis. She could have been named Real Deal, because she exemplified everything a company would want in an employee.

Rill was born three months early, had oxygen complications, and has been blind her whole life. Instead of focusing on what she couldn't do in life, she focused on what she could do. She found work at Memorial Hospital in South Bend as a dark room technician. She thought, "These are the cards I've been dealt in life. I'll play them the best I can. I'm blind. Why not work in a dark room?!"

It was 1999 when I did a TV news inspiration story on her. Rill dutifully showed me all of the things that she did in her job. I could tell she took great pride in her job. She exemplified Excellence in her Job. After showing me her daily routine, she said something that I've always remembered. "When I finish my job I go see if there's anything I can do for anyone else," she said. She exemplified Team Spirit.

I interviewed her supervisor. He said that there were all sorts of construction going on at the hospital but Rill always found her way around it. He just shook his head with admiration. She didn't wander around going, "They should clean this mess up. "They" this. "They" that. She found a way to navigate it every day with a smile on her face.

Of course, how we adapt to change in today's world determines a lot regarding how far we go. Rill is an inspiration there as well. When technology advanced, having dark rooms become a thing of the past in most hospitals. After being a dark room technician for 26 years, that job ended in 2002 as computers took over. Memorial Hospital wanted very much to keep Rill, so everyone worked to see where she could be best utilized. Rill was able to be redeployed in the Market Research Department on patient satisfaction survey mailings.

"I keep the inventory," she said happily. "I stuff the surveys. I love it! I'm extremely lucky I've had two jobs here and have loved both of them! I love life! I absolutely love it!!"

I have used video clips of Rill in motivation training sessions and her story has never ceased to impact people. Her perspective on life is truly exceptional. Her commitment to excellence in attitude, job pride, team spirit, and embracing change is one of the best I have ever seen.

Stokers have such strong attitudes that the little things don't get them all riled up. One of the challenges today is that we sometimes overreact to something someone says or does, and we get a burr under our saddle. We don't shake off a certain comment someone makes, and the next thing you know we're all worked up about it, or them!

Stokers know how to shake certain things off and not let them get to them.

I love the story of the old broken-down mule that fell into the old well. The farmers gathered around the top and said, "The mule is broken down. The well is old and dangerous. We need to fill it in. Tough luck for the mule."

Nice bunch.

The old mule didn't quite pick up on where things were headed until the first shovel full of dirt landed smack on his back. He figured out quickly he was about to get buried. Being a "solutionaholic," he simply started shaking his back as each shovel full of dirt landed on it. Slowly, the dirt built up under his hooves. He rose on up to the top, and walked out with a look of "I may be old and broken down, but you've still got me. Take me back to the farm. A woman mule would be nice after such a stressful day."

That's the way it is in life. There are a lot of things we need to just shake off, and move on.

I shared that mule story one time when speaking to a group of city leaders. Afterwards, a lady went back to her office and started hanging up pictures. I happened to notice, and asked her about it. She said she had been bent out of shape by something someone had done awhile back, but the broken-down mule story showed her she had to shake it off, and move on. She had taken down her pictures as a protest (don't ask me why) and now it was time to hang them back up.

As a man that was on local TV news for years, I used to get recognized a lot when I was out in public. Sometimes folks would know exactly who I was. Other times, they sort of knew! "Hey, there's that guy from the News. He's the, uh, Weather guy, I think." I always nodded as if I was the Weather guy.

Getting recognized can get to you. One time I told two of my children that I had to get out of the viewing area for at least a day. I had to go somewhere where I wouldn't be recognized. So, I got two of our kids and headed down to Kokomo, IN, which was out of the South Bend viewing area. I decided to take them to the Tuesday 2 pm movie show at one of the Kokomo theaters. My kids and I walked in the darkened theater a few minutes before 2 pm. There appeared to be about seven people in there. All of the sudden, they started clapping and pointing at us! I was like, "My gosh, they recognize me HERE!" In Kokomo!"

I shrugged and told my kids to sit down. "Daddy is a big star down here in Kokomo, kids. I need to go meet my fans, sign their popcorn boxes, and all of that. I'll be right back."

I walked over to them and said, "Well, I guess you recognize me from the WSBT news. You must be fans. What can I sign for you." I was like Ted Baxter from the Mary Tyler Moore Show!

One of the guys looked at me with a puzzled, irritated look. He said, "Buddy, I don't know who you are…"

I looked back him somewhat confused.

"All I know," he continued, "was that the people that run this movie theater said that they wouldn't start the 2 pm movie unless at least ten people showed up, and you and your kids make ten!"

There's a piece of humble pie!

I'll let you in on a little motivational speaker secret. First, that's not a real story. Second, I heard former Miami Dolphins coach Don Shula share that story at a benefit dinner for the Boys and Girls Club. It got a great laugh. I stole that sucker, tailored it to my location, and have used it ever since.

Don't tell Don.

The point I was getting at was that I was recognized a ton as a TV news guy. The comment I got more than any other over the years, and I'm talking thousands of times, was this: "Charlie, we watch you for your enthusiasm. You really look like you love what you do. We really like your energy and enthusiasm."

Enthusiasm. Loving what you do.

I am a miser by nature. This drives my wife nuts because she is much looser with the pocketbook than Scrooge Charlie. When it comes to tipping, I have issues when the service isn't top quality. The whole tipping thing is confounding. Some people get tipped, like waiters and hair stylists. Others don't, like news anchors. Hey, if an anchor delivers a flawless newscast, why can't their be a pipe from the viewers home to the anchors desk where the viewers could stuff a few dollar bills and, "WHOOSH," shoot it downtown to the TV station. It would be like those clear pipes at bank drive-throughs where you shoot your money into the teller.

Maybe not.

A few years ago my family stopped at a restaurant in, ironically, Kokomo. Being miser man, I was making sure all of our 436 kids (we have six) ordered ice water and not pop (Coke if your from the South). Our waiter was one of the most genuinely enthusiastic people I had ever seen. I mean this guy was filled with a radiant enthusiasm. He had a bounce in his step and deep care for his customers. He kept checking on us and went above and beyond the call of waiter duty! How good was he? I wanted to tip him during the meal. For a miser, that's a miracle. That's the power of genuine enthusiasm!

It can be hard to stay enthusiastic facing grave challenges in life, but it's very possible to put an enthusiastic perspective on anything. As someone who studies peak performance for my career, I am constantly observing how high achievers deal with all situations in life. When I watch TV, I watch for biography shows and interview shows. One night I watched a long sit-down interview with actor Michael J. Fox, who talked about his battle with Parkinson's disease. He was asked how he kept his attitude up as it attacked his body over the years. Fox said was once in a group where everyone wrote their biggest challenge in life on a piece of white circular paper. Everyone in the group would then stepped towards the middle and lay down their piece of paper. They then stepped back and read everyone else's major challenge.

Fox said that after seeing everyone else's major challenge, his was far from the worst.

Stokers understand perspective. They are also possibility thinkers! When something comes to them, they don't immediately start thinking of all the reasons not to pursue it. It doesn't mean they do pursue it, but they receive things with a "possibility minded" perspective.

Early in my speaking career, I developed a motivational program for athletes. I approached several large schools about the benefits it would have for their athletes. I was met with these responses:

"We don't have the budget for that."

"We don't have time for a speaker at our athletic banquet."

They were polite, but I could tell from the second I told them what I was offering, the answer was going to be "no."

I happened to call one of the tiniest schools in the area, Oregon-Davis High School. I thought that based on the other conversations, this little bitty school wouldn't be signing up for the program. Travis Hannah answered the phone. He was the athletic director and boy's basketball coach. I told him of the program and the benefits. I then listened for the reasons for him not to bring it in. Instead, he responded this way:

"Charlie, I like that program. I think that could have a lasting impact on our kids. They need to hear that message. It addresses some concerns we've had down here."

I almost dropped the phone. "Well, Travis," I said. "The program costs such and such amount." I thought that would be the end of that.

"That's fine," he said. "We don't have that in our budget, but I know our athletic Booster Club would help. If not, I know an individual booster that would cover it." Travis then went on to suggest I deliver the program in a seminar form at the end of the school day instead of at the banquet. I sat there and marveled at his "possibility" way of thinking, and how he suggested to me a more effective way of presenting the program.

Let me tell you a little more about Travis Hannah. He had taken over an Oregon-Davis High School boys basketball team that had lost 56 games in a row. With his possibility-minded approach to everything, he soon had them going the other direction. They started winning games. Within four years he guided them to the State Championship in basketball-mad Indiana.

You cannot tell me his approach to everything in life was not a major factor in Oregon-Davis going from 56 losses in a row to a state championship in a few short seasons. Does being a "possibility minded" person mean Travis Hannah says yes to everything? No. Had I called and said I had a motivational program where I brought dancing kangaroo's down to his school, he would have politely said no. But the difference between him and many of the other athletic directors I talked to was his initial reaction to my proposal. He considered the possibilities, not the difficulties. He found a way to make it happen.

He accomplished his mission at tiny Oregon-Davis, and was gobbled up by a larger school, John Glenn High School, to coach their team.

Stokers do their dandiest to look at the bright side of things. The perspective we take on every situation in life has a great bearing on our performance. I have lived in South Bend, IN for many years. It's a wonderful place to raise a family. The four seasons are beautiful, although the winters can get "rather chilly." One time there was a stretch of days in the seven-degree range that was driving everyone nuts. I stuck to this perspective: "When this bone chilling stretch is over, temperatures in the 30's will seem like summer." Sure enough, when it got to the 30's, it felt great. I went jogging! It all had to do with perspectives during the challenging weather times.

If you have a flat tire, be grateful you have a jack and spare.

One of the top challenges in 21st-century life is keeping a positive attitude. People read books. They go to keynotes and seminars. They come away with improved attitudes. Then, they want to keep their attitudes "up." I often get asked about how to keep a good attitude. My response is to develop daily habits that keep the good attitude cycle going.

One of the most important things I do is have Quiet Time in the morning. It sets the foundation for the day ahead. People say, "Well, it's hard to make time in the morning. I have to hit the floor running!" Well, my wife and I have six children between us. I find a way every day to have quiet time. People say, "How do you find time to do that with six kids?" I answer, "How do I NOT find the time! I need it!"

I observed my father start his days with quiet time. I would come upstairs to get on the school bus and find him at the kitchen table with his Bible, coffee and pipe. Yeah, I know. The pipe thing doesn't fit in with Stokers, but that's what he did. Speaking of which, I chuckle when I recall when my Dad and his wife Annette would have company over at night to visit. They'd go through at least a couple of cups of coffee after 7 pm. How they went to sleep is beyond me.

Back to my point. My dad's quiet time made an impact on me. I have done it for years and used it to set the foundation for the day and the challenges and adventures ahead. I combine prayer and Bible reading, and then I go to the newspaper. I look for stories on inspirational people with great attitudes. I never fail to find at least three or four stories that focus on remarkable people. I read their quotes carefully. What makes them tick? Where do they get their drive from in life? How have they overcome adversity? You see, I am feeding my positive attitude cycle. I am pouring more fuel into it. A positive attitude has to be maintained. I cannot emphasize enough how much value I get from morning quiet time and pin pointing certain stories in the morning paper.

I love to give timely examples. I am writing this part of this chapter on Sept. 19, 2007. In the Sept. 18th edition of the *South Bend Tribune,* where I live, I focused my reading on a front page story on a young man named Mark O'Dell at Washington High School. He had scored a perfect 2400 on his SAT. I went through the story to read his quotes. I looked to see what it had to say about his parents and their impact on him. I then kept going through the paper and found a story on Hannah Dover, a third-grader at Queen of Peace Catholic School. Over the past two years she had asked that friends and family not give her birthday presents. Instead, she asked that they donate money to Hannah and Friends foundation. Her incredible generosity had led to over $1500 going to charity. You think that didn't boost my attitude for the day and send me off with a giving spirit! My attitude was refueled by a third grader that sacrifices her birthday material things so that a home for adults with special needs can benefit.

People say, "I don't have time to read the paper." It is time challenging to go through the whole thing, but when you get a knack of finding the inspirational stories in the paper, your attitude each day will improve.

The pile of work dumped on many people today borders on ridiculous. Mountains of tasks wait to be done. While quiet time in the morning sets the foundation, there's still a lot of the day left! One thing I've done over the years is use drive time to focus on blessings and encouraging things that I can to others throughout the day. Also, whenever I have the midday meal (or sandwich on the run)

I try to do a 5. By that I mean I take 5 slow, deep breaths before eating. I think peaceful thoughts.

Some folks that are pressed for time at lunch can fire off a machine gun prayer that goes along the lines of: "ThankyoudearGodforthisfoodandthisday.Amen" Chomp. Chomp. Chomp.

I don't believe that's the most effective route . . .

At first the 5 can drive you crazy, especially if you're high strung and a "go go go" person. Stick with it. The world won't rush by as you are doing the 5. It can be settling.

One of the seminars I am developing on Attitude builds around the importance of developing a Circle of Thought. We all benefit from taking the time to write down a list of motivational quotes that really stand out to us, scripture, poetry, special moments, and things of that nature. Then, when our attitudes are challenges, we go back to the Circle of Thought and keep going around and around it until we get back on track on pointed in that direction.

Stokers have the ability to put the right perspective on everything in life. They also have the ability to have what I call "Initial Spin." It's how you first shape everything that comes at you. It's important, because it sets the tone. It forms the foundation for the attitudes that will follow.

There is the story of the English family in World War II that scampered into their bomb shelter as Nazi planes approached. As they huddled under the ground, the planes destroyed their home. Upon emerging the father held his family as he stared at a huge crater where their house used to stand.

"I've always wanted a basement," he said. "Now we have the foundation to build one!"

That's initial spin. He took as positive of a perspective that he possible could. His wife may have shot him a look like he was loopy, but he knew his family needed an initial positive spin. I can relate. Several years ago a tornado barreled through the woods behind our home. It uprooted a beech tree like a toothpick and slammed it right on our roof. The damage was significant. The roof was destroyed. Limbs shot into our bedroom. Water damage ran through the house. We were looking at months of rebuilding.

Upon racing home and seeing the damage I turned to my wife and said, "Our roof was old and badly needed new tiles. With six kids, we had wondered how we were going to be able to afford it. This will make it possible."

Don't tell the insurance man I said that.

Call me a hopeless optimist who looks at everything through rose-tinted glasses, but that initial spin helped keep me sane over months of workers trudging through the house and nights spent sleeping on a mattress on the floor!

There was once a church that suffered tremendous damage in a fire. The congregation gathered with great sadness. They had reason to be down. The pastor realized their despair and used Initial Spin (although I would imagine he had a better term for it) at that critical time. He predicted that the fire damage would bring the people closer together as they rebuilt. And it did. He predicted that it would bring in new members. And it did. People who had been thinking about going to the church suddenly showed up. He predicted this awful event would actually help the youth group, which didn't have large numbers. And it did. The youth formed a musical praise band called "After the Fire."

Stokers process things with an initial positive spin that builds on their commitment and determinate to reach excellence. Sometimes it means rolling up the sleeves right away and getting down working to solving the problem. Sometimes it means building everyone else up with "glass half full" logic. Whatever the case, they don't roll their eyes and show any signs of exasperation. They know that a lot of life will be "a bear" and the perspective they take for the challenge is critical to beating it!

If you want to earn a doctorate in perspectives, strive to be like the fellow who went to Las Vegas with his wife. He left their room to go down to play a little roulette. He took two dollars with him. He laid a bet, and won. He kept winning and winning to the tune of $50,000. He started to head back up to the room when he decided to do one more double or nothing roll. The winning streak ended with a thud. The $50,000 was gone. As he walked back into their room his wife looked up and asked, "How did you do?"

"I lost two dollars."

Now, that's perspective!

"A pessimist sees the difficulty in every opportunity; an optimist sees the opportunity in every difficulty."
   Winston Churchill

"When things are going rough, think of this thought: 'I could be a bump on a pickle.' Realizing that you are not a lowly bump on a pickle will make you feel better about your current lot in life."
   Charlie Adams

CHAPTER 10

YOU CAN DO
ANYTHING – ALMOST

One of the popular motivational things to say is, "You can do anything." We say that to young people and it truly does inspire many of them. But sometimes it can be a bit silly. I mean, take the hypothetical case of a 43 year old squatty 5'2" man that comes up to me and says, "Charlie, I can do anything. I am going to be a center for the Lakers in the N.B.A." I would look at him and say, "No. No, you're not. You would not fare well against 7'9" Yao Ming. You could be President, though."

Can we do anything? Not quite, but we can do a whole bunch of things! In 23 years of being in TV News, I took away one especially powerful motivating tool. Being in that business showed me that all of us are capable of doing just about anything. You see, newscasts are live. They have to be ready to go. An anchor can't pop up on the screen at 11:00 pm and say, "Excuse us, viewers. We're not quite ready yet. We'll start the newscast in just a few minutes." I've gone to plays that advertise starting at 8 pm and start at 8:06. Weddings that proclaim a 2 pm start get going at 2:03. Not TV news. That newscast starts right on the money every time year after year.

There was a time our live newscast at WSBT TV in South Bend was less than a minute away from starting. The editor finished laying down the final piece of video on the story as the producer yelled through his headset that the tape had to be upstairs in 30 seconds. I happened to be walking by the editing room. The editor, who was in his late 50's, realized he didn't have Olympic speed and there was no way he was getting his rear up the stairs in time. He looked at me and saw a 6' 6" man in his late 30's who was in good shape.

"Here, you take the tape up!"

I took off like a rocket. At the stairs I took five steps at a time with my long strides. Had I taken three steps, I would not have made it. I burst into the control room with the tape 12 seconds before air time. The tape operator loaded the tape and it ran right on time at 11 pm. As I walked back I looked at the steps that I had just glided over and wondered how the heck did I take five of those at a time? It was because at the time I had to in order to achieve success.

Stokers rise, sometimes literally, to the occasion. They do it because it's exciting! They don't explain it. It just happens.

Stokers don't limit themselves. They realize they can do almost anything. I once heard former football star Desmond Howard deliver a talk. He recalled when he played for the Green Bay Packers. It was the night before their Super Bowl matchup against the New England Patriots. Desmond was in his hotel room reflecting on the big day ahead when there was a knock on his door. It was representative of Disney. They were going room to room reminding players that if they ended up being named Most Valuable Player then the Disney film crew would ask them the famous question.

"Hey, so and so, you just won the Super Bowl. Where are you going now?"

If you've seen the commercial, the player always says, "Disney World!"

Desmond happened to be on a team that was built around superstars Brett Favre and Reggie White. Surely, they would end up being in the commercial. Desmond could have chuckled and wondered why they were even bothering coming to his room. But he didn't limit himself. He ended up having a terrific game the next day, and changed the momentum of the game with a big return. He was named MVP! He did the Disney commercial!

As a Peak Performance specialist, I am constantly reading about high achievers and listening to what they have to say. In May of 2007 I happened to watch a report leading up to the Indy 500. Danica Patrick, the first woman ever to lead a lap at the historic race, was being interviewed. She said something that made me sit up. She said that we can do anything we set our minds to, especially when it is our passion. Bingo! I thought she nailed it with that clarification. When I speak to young people I hammer home that important part of the equation. To overcome the obstacles to be whatever it is you want to be, it almost has to be your passion or eventually you will wear down.

When I went into sportscasting as a young man, it was my passion. I achieved every goal I ever set as a sportscaster. I traveled the world and interviewed countless high achievers. Did I make a lot of money? Not really, but every day I drove to work I was chomping at the bit to get there to take on the challenges and opportunities of the day! I did it until the fire within in me started to burn out. I had promised myself I wouldn't give viewers a charred version of myself, so I left and followed my new passion: motivational keynotes and training sessions. A new flame of passion had been ignited.

I used to do a segment on the news called "Challenge Charlie." Viewers challenged me to their area of expertise. I would go out and get embarrassed, but it made for fun television. It also taught viewers how important it is to follow your passion. I did a story on a young lady who was one of the best disc golfers in America. She could take that Frisbee-looking disc and gracefully launch it at a target 75 yards away. The disc would gently land right at the base. Even though I was much bigger and stronger than she, I was a joke when it came to competing against her. It was a thing of beauty to watch her throw that disc.

It was her passion. She didn't make much money, but equipment sponsors took her around the nation to competitions. She loved what she did, so much to where she had become the best in the nation at it!

I learned a great deal from those "Challenge Charlie" segments. I once had a girl bowler challenge me to come out and play her. I knew I was in trouble when she arrived to the lanes with several balls and special bowling gloves. As we played, she changed balls based on the oil situation on the lanes! I just had a ball I have found on the rack. It fit my fingers. That seemed good to me!

As we played, I learned that bowling was her passion and she hoped to earn a partial college scholarship in the sport. She also had an incredible work ethic regarding the sport. She practiced daily, and one night spent almost two hours practicing one shot over and over on a particular pin placement.

One time an elementary student challenged me to come out and play him in table tennis. I call it ping pong, but table tennis is the term these days. I arrived as a 41-year-old man. This kid was in grade school. I looked at him like Goliath looked at David. "This is who you send to play me in ping pong?!" I really thought I would smoke his tail. Instead, I don't think I ever got a point on the kid. He had this funky serve where he could put different spins on the ball. I looked like Otis the town drunk from Andy Griffith as I tried to hit the confounded little white ball back. He tore me up!

As I interviewed him I learned that he practiced ten to twenty hours a week! He truly sought to be one of the best in the nation and the world in his sport. He was doing it! I am often brought into to speak to young people about the dangers of underage drinking. One community in Missouri had me come to speak to their high school students.

There had been twelve alcohol related deaths in the last five years involving kids in school or just out of school. One of the reasons was that some kids thought the small community "was boring."

I tell kids there are no boring places. You may be a boring person. If a young person lives in such a so-called "boring community" then by all means take up a passion like those kids that challenged me on the news. The elementary student that mastered table tennis spent his idle hours crafting different serves that challenged the laws of physics. Peak Performers find their passion and hone it, whether they live in Morgan City, MS (population 250) or Los Angeles.

When I speak to young people, I try to pound home a simple formula for their success in life. Find your passion and work it hard! When you find your passion, the rest won't even seem like work, and your attitude will be great because you are doing what you love.

Likes thousands of people, I am a big Zig Ziglar fan. He has a story where he says a positive at-titude doesn't mean you can do anything, but it means you can do a whole lot more than if you have a negative attitude. "Ain't that the truth?", as my Aunt Betty in Oxford, Mississippi would say.

Stokers truly can't do anything they set out to do. There are some limits, but they can do almost anything as long as it is their passion, and their positive attitude outweighs their negative attitude.

Early in my professional speaking and training days, I happened to talk to a woman who coaches speakers. She had known Ziglar for years, and had helped coach him in his early days of speaking. As we were talking on the phone, this lady changed subjects and revealed powerful insight to me.

"You know, Charlie," she said. "When Zig Ziglar gave himself wholeheartedly to God, his speaking career took off. From that day forward he never had to pursue a speaking engagement again. They kept flowing in." She shared the same insight regarding another speaker, Keith Harrell, who is one of America's top Attitude speakers. Her point wasn't that they went on to do very well financially, although that was part of it. She simply dropped in that juggernaut of wisdom while sharing other coaching insights.

"Just remember, you can do anything you set your mind to, but it takes action, perseverance, and facing your fears."
    Gillian Anderson

CHAPTER 11

STOKING AS AN ORGANIZATION

Stokers are saturated with team and organization spirit. They exude it. It comes out of their pores.

Companies and organizations that bring in the *Stoke the Fire Within* message often ask me to emphasize Team Building. They will say that they have an inordinate amount of people willing to bellyache about certain things, but who aren't willing are capable of coming up with solutions. "We need more solution-centered thinking," they will say to me.

A Stoker is a more than solution-centered person. A Stoker is a "Solution Freak" when it comes to challenges. They're not crazy about problems, but when they happen they immediately relish the opportunity to come up with a lasting solution. They have no interest in wasting time pointing fingers. For many years, I was not a solutionaholic. I would mope and snort and stomp if things went wrong. I fired off a few "they should do this" or "they should do that" until I finally got it. I converted into being a "Solution Freak" and found it to be actually fun! Think about it. How often do we get to be a freak about anything? Why not be a Solution Freak?

In my TV newsdays, I put a lot of effort into producing a three-minute sportscast. It usually took several hours. I wanted it to go well, especially since thousands of people were watching at home. One time during the 6 pm News I walked out onto the set during the weather segment. I sat down off camera and put on my wireless microphone. The weather segment ended and commercials started airing for a couple of minutes. The anchors and the floor crew started chatting about things. As a result, the floor director forgot the normal procedure of asking for an "audio check" from my wireless microphone. The commercials ended and I began the live sportscast. I started yapping away, but no one at home heard me. That's because the battery was dead in my microphone.

It took half a minute to clarify the problem, then a minute for the floor people to get another microphone, then another 15 clumsy seconds of my trying to fit it on, and the sportscast went down the commode. It was a train wreck.

Was it disappointing? Yes! Like any Stoker, I was committed and determined to reach excellence, so I was hurt as I walked back to the office. But, I quickly went into "Solution Freak" mode. A Stoker does everything he or she can to make sure mistakes never happen again.

From that day on, I always said "Audio test... check...test 1-2-3...audio test" as I put on the microphone during the commercials before the sports segment. The floor director was usually great at checking the microphone, but this way I made sure we had it tested.

The microphone problem never happened again.

Any organization that gets everyone together and pumps up the Solution Freak approach will benefit. When a problem arises, everyone should start doing back flips over the excitement of coming up with the solution. Okay. Okay. That's asking a lot! But seriously, no one wants to hear someone bellyache about a problem and point fingers all over the place. People do want to hear sensible ways to solve the problem.

I was a Sports Director for almost two decades for local TV news stations. My department was constantly understaffed and always faced budget restraints. Over time, I came to relish the Solution Freak approach to every challenge.

Covering Friday night high school sports actually is

a top priority of stations across America. The idea is to get as many camera people out as possible to cover as many games as possible. That translates to a lot of Momma's, Poppa's and Aunt Linda's watching that night. I always tried to get five or six camera people out in the field to various games. We set a goal of 14 games. One year, however, we went through staffing challenges and faced a stretch of weeks with only three or four camera people. That's a significant drop in production.

I could have lamented that the competition was going to kick our tails, but I took the Solutionaholic approach. I brainstormed and came up with another approach. We would still cover the most important games, but there was no way to be all over creation. So, I assigned one camera person to stay at one game in its entirety. He was to be in both locker rooms before the game to get the coaches pre game talks. He was to go get what the coaches said at halftime, and after the game. He then was to come back and put together a fairly long documentary-type piece for the show that night.

It turned out to be a big hit with viewers!

We had one game where one coach was all wound up in his pre-game talk, while the other coach played soothing symphony music to his players. The viewers ate it up. They totally forgot, or didn't

care, that we weren't at 14 games. They loved seeing the personalities of the coaches and the halftime adjustments and the raw emotions of going
behind the scenes!

By being Solution Freaks, we were able to take a
negative and make it a positive!

One of the great challenges of organizations is the
constant "they shoulds" that are said around water
coolers and around the corners of hallways. "They
should do this" or "they should do that."

Stokers are constantly aware of the "they" word.
They monitor themselves on it constantly. They see
no value in taking part of "they should do this" at
any time. If they use the "they" word then it's in a
form of praise.

In Team Building sessions I have groups recite a
"they" vow. It's a lot of fun. The goal is to make
everyone aware of how self defeating the "they
should" nonsense is to a team. I'm realistic, though.
I encourage them to cut down on the "they should"
talk. Let's be honest. In today's world it's hard not
to get frustrated and let out an occasional "they
should!"

If a person finds themselves spouting off "they
shoulds" a lot and is generally miserable with their
position, they need to reflect. Did they end up in

that position because someone at the company lassoed them on the street and dragged them in saying, "Yeehaw, you are going to be miserable here and point fingers a lot! Now, start your job!"

That would be justification for bellyaching. However, in most cases it takes reflection and applying the "No More" approach to why the person is in such a bellyaching position.

Stokers exude team in everything that they do. They lead the way. As leaders, it's important to set the example. I once spoke to the Polygon Company, which is as an engineered materials company. Their H.R. director, Dan McMillion, was telling me of the time they had a massive order. The deadline to getting it out was fast approaching. The owners of the company rolled up their shirt sleeves and started stacking fiber glass and whatever else it took to get the job done! They made it!

Earlier in this book I wrote about Kenny McCreary, who went from part- time room service delivery person to management at The Summit Club of South Bend, IN, one of the nicest restaurants in the Midwest. I spoke with him about Team one time and he passionately shared his recipe for success as a leader in that area. He led by example. He always arrived to work impeccably dressed to manage the team. However, if the cleaning person had called in sick, he immediately took off his nice suit jacket, rolled up his sleeves, and went to work making sure the bathroom was spotless for the customers. If a server couldn't be there, he pitched in and helped in that job.

"By working hard and doing whatever it takes," he told me, "everyone else wants to work hard. When they see me, the leader, doing all these things, it makes them want to work hard."

Stokers enhance organization unity by planning on a daily basis to say encouraging things to fellow team members. I'm not talking about bouncing around the room like Richard Simmons saying "You're special" and "You're a winner" and "Go get 'em, Bobby!" That's over the top and, to be honest, annoys me. What Stokers do is have a game plan to say something encouraging to a specific person that is thoughtful and meaningful.

For example, in TV newsI worked with a lot of young News reporters. They'd come out of college all fired up and rarin' to go. Management would mean well, but would often focus on the negatives of their reports from that day's newscast. I could see a little slumping of the shoulders in the young reporter. I made it a habit to watch their reports and later praise them about a specific point.

You could see their face just light up.

As a speaker, I have greatly benefited from encouragement from audience members. When I speak, I get a variety of expressions from folks. There will be stern looks from those who are very focused on the content. There will be looks that say, "Who the hell is this speaker and what does he know that I don't know." There will be smiling faces and faces that look like they should have gone to the bathroom at the last break. Then there will be the nodding faces. They represent encouragement. In my talk, I could say "leave here and start raising monkeys and you will make millions" and those particular audience members would nod. It's not that they agree with such a point, but that they are encouragers. They are encouraging me. As a result I find myself looking back at them several times during the talk. I feed off their encouragement.

I mainly speak in corporate and academic settings, but also am asked to speak in church settings. The first few times I did so I got to thinking of such-and-such sin here and such-and-such sin there, and I wondered if God might throw a lightning bolt down and char my butt as I spoke in His house. Inevitably, I would see the calming face of a little old lady nodding at whatever I said, and that strengthened me. Every thirty seconds I would look back at that lady. I drew off her encouragement.

It's been said that encouragement costs nothing to give, but is priceless to receive.

The next time you are driving to work or an activity, spend that time specifically thinking of something encouraging you are going to say to a particular person. You will play a significant part of their day, and your team will grow. Who knows? When they die they're liable to leave you millions of dollars. I'm just saying . . .

William Arthur Ward, the author of *Fountains of Faith*, once said, "Flatter me and I may not believe you. Criticize me and I may not like you. Ignore me and I may not forgive you. Encourage me and I will not forget you." I believe Ward had many insightful things to say over the years that can be of great value to Stokers. Here is another remarkable observation: "Do more than belong: participate. Do more than care: help. Do more than believe: practice. Do more than be fair: be kind. Do more than forgive: forget. Do more than dream: work."

Stokers help others in the organization by helping them raise their level of competition through challenge. It is good to encourage. It's also good to challenge.

A young man named Ryne Lightfoot entered his freshman year at Bethel College with a determination to challenge his teammates. In preseason conditioning drills he refused to ever come in second place. The team darted from baseline to baseline. If Ryne found someone close to him in the sprint to the finish, he would literally throw his body across the finish line. He would crash to the hardwood floor screaming!

Think that didn't inspire his teammates?

Each day he would walk around going, "Who's going to beat me today? Anyone?" He didn't do it in a cocky way. It was his way as a Stoker of helping the team raise its level of determination and competitiveness.

Stokers embrace helping others in the organization. I heard former football player Dan Dierdorf speak at the College Football Hall of Fame one time. Dierdorf had starred at Michigan and in the NFL. He said to have your teammates say you made them better is the ultimate complement. To have them say they learned from your work ethic, mindset, and availability is the ultimate sign of a team person.

Back in my TV newsdays, I aired a weekly segment called "This Week's Outstanding Student

Athlete." One particular week we honored a volleyball player named Candice Obregon. We contacted her to let her know we would be sending a crew out to interview her. She got right back with us and thanked us for the honor. She also said there was a player on the team that she felt should be honored before her. She said the other player was a "setter" on the team and meant more to the team. She went on and on about that other player. I thought to myself, "Candice is a true team player."

Earlier in this book in the chapter on Separating Yourself, I wrote about a young lady named Elaine Hessel. She was the one who came up with the idea of improving her basketball rebounding skills by having her dad throw the ball off their uneven grain bin roof. Besides separating herself in regards to Peak Performance, she also showed a remarkable passion for team.

In December of her senior basketball season at Plymouth High School in northern Indiana, she tore the ACL of her knee in practice. In the blink of an eye, her season was over. Her State Championship hopes were gone. It is hard for any of us to understand how difficult it is for a premier athlete to lose their senior season of high school sports, especially when they were picked as a State Championship favorite. There were plenty of tears in her home that night because her high school basketball career had ended so abruptly.

How unfair. She had worked harder than anyone. But she knew life could be unfair and she knew much of life is how we respond to adversity. She couldn't choose her circumstances, but she could choose how she responded. Not reacted, but responded. What Elaine did is an example all of us "grown folks" can learn from.

The next day the Plymouth JV and Varsity teams played games. It was only natural to think Elaine would remain home on her injured knee. Who would have blamed her for throwing a pity party for days? Instead, the gym doors opened, and Elaine slowly moved across the court. She humbly assembled the team video camera gear and taped the JV game. She then helped coach the varsity game.

She had set a limit on how long she would be down. She then gritted her teeth and got about the business of making the most out of her situation. She did so by focusing on what she could do for others. Think about it. Elaine was the holder of eight school records. She was a high school All American candidate. Yet, she wasn't above videotaping the junior varsity game.

She later told me, "We all have roles on a team. My role had changed dramatically. It didn't mean I wasn't a part of the team anymore. I was going to do whatever I could to help."

Elaine was no longer the leading scorer and rebounder. She now was dedicated to supporting others. That's what she did. She was awarded with a scholarship to Indiana Wesleyan University to play basketball and study Nursing.

This kind of "Team Saturated Spirit" applies to any occupation. She inspired her teammates in a great way. They went on to have a better season than many thought they could.

Dean Smith was a legendary basketball coach at the University of North Carolina. He would have been a successful CEO in any business. He built his championship program on TEAM. The great Michael Jordan played for him, and totally bought into the team-first philosophy. It helped him win a national championship as a college player. Smith started something that I think could work in any business. After his players scored a basket, they would run back down the court to play defense. As they ran back down the court they were to point at the person that had passed them the ball to set up their basket. It was to say "you made the basket possible."

That doesn't just have to happen on the basketball court. They say pointing is not polite, but in this case it's a good thing. In the office you could develop a practice of pointing a coworkers who have stepped up and made successful things happen. You could have all kinds of fun with it. The day could be filled with pointing! Meetings could be juiced up with a pointing session!

It took me awhile as a professional to totally embrace Team. Back when I was a sportscaster on local TV News, I used to "hoard" my sports time. I generally got three minutes out of the 6 pm newscast. By golly, that was my three minutes and I wanted it!

Zig Zigler has a message that to get what you want, it's important to get others what they want. By helping them, you help yourself. For years, I bucked that logic. For example, when stormy weather would hit the viewing area the producer of the newscast would come to me asking me to give up some of my time in the sportscast. Based on my reaction, you would have thought they were coming to take some of my teeth.

"Ohhh, noooo," I would grumble.

The producer would shrug his or her shoulders and move on. I would sit there like a selfish child that got his way. Eventually, I got it, and saw the light! When I learned of impending bad weather, I would go to the producer first! I would say, "Hey, I hear there's bad weather coming. You'll need more time for weather in the newscast. Please take a minute of my sportscast time. Also, do you need to use any of the sports guys to go out with a camera and shoot weather video?

The producer would look at me like I needed to be checked for a fever. Was this the same guy who used to hoard his sports time and not be a true team player?! I had changed. I was saturated with team spirit!

The result was remarkable. The next time I would need extra time on a busy night in sports, the producer of the newscast was more than willing to help out. The generosity was back and forth. We wanted to help each other. The team benefited!

Stokers always recognize everyone that plays a role in the success of the team. They don't have to be a leader to make sure the "behind the scenes" people are appreciated. Having covered teams and organizations in News and Sports for years, I am here to tell you that the value of the "behind the scenes" people is critical for success.

As I mentioned, we put together a highly successful Friday Night High School Sports show for years. It brought in tremendous revenue to the station and a lot of new viewers to sample the news product. I was the host which meant I was the so called "star" of the show. Thousands of people knew me as "Chopper Charlie" because I flew around to games in a helicopter.

My approach was that, like everyone else, I was one part of the well- oiled machine. I appreciated everyone, and needed everyone – especially those that filled the "Linda" role.

Every successful organization has a Linda. They wouldn't be successful without them.

While I got the glory of swooping around in a helicopter, Linda got the grunt work of working with schools to determine exactly where the helicopter could land. Baseball outfield. Soccer field. Was it secured? How would open the gate lock? Can't land there? How about the nearby hospital landing pad? Who would drive Charlie from there to the field? Phone calls. Faxes. More phone calls. Signed faxes. On and on.

Then there was the matter of where we would land when we came back to the station. Because the TV station was in the heart of downtown South Bend, there was no station landing pad. Linda went to work. She hammered the phones to work with the City of South Bend. Finally she came up with a solution. We would land on a parking garage downtown. But wait! There were insurance issues. City issues. How would we get from the top of the parking garage back to the station? Would the garage be open that late at night?

She did it all with a smile on her face.

As a Stoker, I made sure to thank her every week.

Who are the Linda's on your team and in your organization? Have you thanked them and appreciated them lately. When I speak at company awards banquets I often watch as they award Top Producer awards and Employee of the Year awards and watches to retiring employees, but what about a "Linda" award? Find someone in the history of your organization that has been a Super Linda, and name the award after them. Then, each year award it to a key behind the scenes person. Of course in today's hyper-sensitive world you have to be careful you don't offend someone, but it's worth pursuing. Linda's are critical to team success!

"Encouragement is the oxygen of the soul."
  George Adams

CHAPTER 12

STOKERS ARE UNSTOPPABLE

In June of 2007 I led an Edgerton's Travel group motivational/inspirational tour to the Colorado Rockies by Train. One of our stops was at the Olympic Training Center in Colorado Springs. It was there that I experienced one of the strongest motivational moments of my life.

We had a very enthusiastic and knowledgeable young lady for a guide. She took us around the center and showed us all kinds of interesting things. We saw female volleyball players who averaged 6'1" in height. We saw the rifle range, the living area, the aquatics center, and much more. Towards the end of the tour we came to the weight room. My first observation was that it was not a Taj Mahal weight room. It was serviceable, but certainly not like some of the weight rooms you see in college football programs.

There was a glass wall area where we could observe the Olympic candidates busting their tails. As we started to leave the area someone in our group looked up at the ceiling.

"What's that there for?' the tourist asked the guide.

"Oh, you mean that fence material?" the guide replied. We all looked up at a rather odd sight. A fence had been put up at the top of the walls right where the walls connected with the ceiling tiles. It had been done efficiently, but definitely had the look of construction done fairly recently. It sort of looked like someone had been sent out to Home Depot to find supplies that would fix a problem that had unexpectedly developed.

Their "problem" was the athletes – the dedicated Olympic candidate athletes who sought excellence in all that they do. The guide explained that many of the athletes were so dedicated to improvement that they were constantly on fire to do more cardio-vascular, or come back for another set of weights to isolate calf muscles, or anything to get a little better. They were coming back at all hours, even when the weight room was closed in the middle of the night.

Did that deter them? No. They were committed and determined to reach excellence. C + D = E. They would arrive to find the weight room locked. Instead of turning away, they got something to stand on, knocked out the ceiling tiles, and climbed through to the weight room. They dropped down, and went to work.

Organizers had to put up fencing to keep them out!

I sat there for a minute and got misty eyed. What can I say? I'm a motivational guy. I thought that there are so many people in this world that will do anything to get out of extra work, and these athletes were crawling through walls and dropping into weight rooms to work out even more!

That's Peak Performance! That's stoking the fire within! Many of these athletes won't ever make it, but that doesn't matter. They're dedicated to becoming the best they can! If you want to be the best, you are going to have to knock out some ceiling tiles in your life.

As I mentioned earlier in this book, when I began my broadcasting career late in college I worked hard all during the week. On weekends, the broadcasting facility would be locked. I didn't knock out the ceiling tiles. University Security would have frowned on that for sure! Instead, I went to engineer Jerry Campbell's house and got the keys. I put in hours and hours of extra work to hone my skills. I set out to be the best sportscaster on local TV news that I could possibly become in life.

I encourage you to be the best ever at what you do, with a curiosity as to who is a distant second.

I encourage you to set a goal that when you die a current or former U.S. President will be at your funeral. Get real, Charlie, you say. Well, my grandfather, Everett Adams, was the Principal/Teacher of a five-teacher school in tiny Bethesda, Mississippi. One of their students was a kid named Buford Ellington. He would go on to become a two time Governor of Tennessee. When Buford died, President Lyndon Johnson attended his funeral. If country boy Buford from Bethesda, Mississippi can live a life that brings a former U.S. President to his funeral, you can too!

I encourage you to reevaluate your Dash. Say what? You've probably heard the motivational story regarding grave markers. There's a birth date and the date of death on just about every tombstone or grave marker. In between the dates there is the tiny "dash." The dash represents your life. That little dash has the capability of holding a whole lot of life in it. How is your dash doing? Where is it boring and listless. Where is it going through the motions? Where is it rocking and rolling? Dash reflection is a good thing. Gather the family around one Sunday evening, pop some popcorn, and have a dash reflection time. You could do it for overall life, or for more recent happenings. Craig and Heidi Tornquist have a wonderful tradition. Every Sunday night they gather their beautiful three girls and everyone reflects on the events of the past week. Their evening starts with Craig making a run to Dairy Queen to fill everyone's special order. When he gets back, "Family Tradition" starts with everyone sharing their favorite parts of the week. Craig says he and his wife look forward to it, and their family grows closer because of it! Craig says that they hardly ever miss one – maybe one a year. They are committed to making it happen. Hey, the C + D = E formula applies to Sunday night family functions as well!

I encourage you to follow Miss Kosciusko's advice. Years ago I delivered a keynote on Leadership in Warsaw, Indiana. Miss Kosciusko, Erin Cassidente, performed some songs (it doesn't get any better than a Leadership Talk with singing!) during the event. In between songs she turned to the audience and shared something she had heard in church recently. She said, "Live your life where the preacher doesn't have to lie at your funeral." That got all of us to thinking! She's right. Have you ever been at a funeral of some fellow who was challenged in the integrity issues, and the preacher carried on like he man had been Sunday school teacher of the Year? You found yourself standing there going, "Is the preacher talking about the same guy I knew?!"

I encourage you to find a place to worship regularly and have fellowship with other believers. Don't wait for six strong men to take you to church.

I encourage you to keep pressing on in life! Stokers keep getting better all the time in every way they can. When they screw up, they figure out why, and charge forward in a way to where they don't do it again – or as much! Stokers don't allow themselves to keep dwelling on past mistakes. It's like driving a car. See how well you do going forward down the road at 45 mph, when you are staring in the rear view mirror! If God had meant us to constantly harp on going backwards, our feet would point the other direction. One time I went deep sea fishing and sat at the back of the boat. Without realizing it, my constant staring at the churning waters off the back of the boat caused me to get as sick as a dog in the afternoon. That's what I got for looking backwards all day!

Stokers will get knocked on their butt in life. There will be challenges, and there will be mighty challenges, but they lock their jaw and keep going! They do not drink the dangerous poison of self pity.

When I was a young boy, my mother enrolled me in the Duke University Basketball Camp. There were several other hundred kids. At the time I hadn't played much basketball. I even wore dark blue church socks one time in a game. I didn't know you were supposed to wear white athletic socks! Early on in the Duke Camp, teams were picked. The captains had seen that I wasn't worth a hoot as a player, so I wasn't picked in the early goings. Or the middle goings. Or deep into the late goings!

The group of several hundred got down to me. I was standing there against the bleachers by myself. The kid that had to pick me had an expression that looked like, "Do I have to take him?" I gritted my teeth and kept working on my basketball skills in the camp and over the years. I never became a regular starter until my last year of high school ball. It was during my senior year that my team was locked in a tight battle in the District Championship game of the Mississippi High School state basketball tournament. The game was tied! The clock wound down and the ball ended up in my hands with five seconds to go. Why it wasn't in the hands of our star, big Cecil Turner, was beyond me. All I knew was the ball was in my hands and I'd better do something with it! I dribbled the ball towards the hoop and scored at the very end. We won the game.

From not being picked at the Duke Camp, to state tournament hero. I hadn't given up!

Ara Parseghian was one of the great coaches in Notre Dame football history. He guided the Fightin' Irish to two National Championships and many victories. In reflecting on his career he said there were two key foundations to their success.

They had no breaking point.

There was no circumstance that they couldn't overcome.

In 1989 I was managing the Sports Department at WSBT TV. A young man named Dean Huppert was a part-time sports reporter for us. He was tested mightily early in his career. He could have broken, but he had no breaking point. He also ran into a circumstance that he overcame, even though it was humiliating.

As a leader of my department, I recognized tremendous heart and passion within Dean. He was from the area and cared deeply, to the third degree, about reporting on the community. Dean hustled everywhere with the camera and did many fine reports for us. However, we had a decision maker in the newsroom at the time that would not let him anchor the sports segment on the evening news under any circumstances. The news director looked at superficial things. He felt Dean's voice "was made for newspaper" and felt his mouth drooped a bit.

There came a time when I had to be on the road reporting on Notre Dame football and the other main guy in Sports had to be in Indianapolis reporting on a major high school game. That left only Dean to anchor the segment back at the station. The decision maker found a way around that possibility. He decided to have a news reporter anchor the sports segment. The only problem was the news reporter openly admitted and joked she knew very little about sports. It was as if the decision maker took delight in the ridiculous nature of the set up. What could Dean do? Well, he did whatever he could to help prepare the sportscast for this lady. He was a professional. He edited her tapes and helped write her scripts. When writing her Cubs highlights script he wrote, "Mark Grace rips a double off the wall." As she read it in practice she asked him to clarify which one was getting to second base and which one was the thing the ball bounced off of. He patiently explained that a double was something where the runner got to the second base, and that the wall was the hard thing the ball bounced off. I think she understood what the wall was, but the "double" thing had her confused.

Sure enough, when she was out there delivering the sportscast live on the air, she said, "Mark Grace rips the wall off the double. The ball bounces off the double and there he goes!" All Dean could do was sit in the sports office and watch it air. It was humiliating to him as he sat there, but he just bit his lip and was as professional as he could be. Peak Performers sometimes get dumped on in life. They just have to wait. Dean never did get the opportunity to advance at the station because of the opinions of one decision maker. He eventually got a chance to move to another station as the weekend sports anchor. Before long he became the main guy there and went on to develop one of the best Friday Night football and basketball shows in local TV news history. He has received the IHSAA Distinguished Service Award, which is the most prestigious media award in Indiana High School sports. He has been committed and determined to reach excellence for years at his station.

And he never says, "There's a wall off the double."

One of the best books I have read in recent years is *Tomorrow Will Start Without* You by Betty Alexander. The Alabama native was the youngest of twelve children. She eventually moved to Indiana to raise her family. In 1994 her grown son Steve was killed instantly by a drunk driver who then sped from the accident. As a parent myself, I can't imagine the hurt and anguish Betty went through after the tragedy. She said her faith and the help of others sustained her.

Four years later police arrived at her home again. Her grown son Jimmy had been killed by a drunk driver. Both sons had died within blocks of her home. The news was initially devastating to her, but both times she clung deeply to her faith. The pain was still as deep as a canyon, but she persevered. Betty started taking classes at Interfaith Christian University and graduated in 2001 with a certificate of achievement at age 68! Today she speaks to groups and officiates over weddings and funerals.

"Life goes on even at my age," she writes in her book. "And I know there are greater things in store for me. I can do all things through Jesus Christ who strengthens me."

I met Betty a few years ago and see her every so often. There is a fire within her! She is a battler. She had been knocked to the ground harder than anyone hit by Mike Tyson in his prime. Her recovery often took a long time, but she always recovered and kept going!

You hear talk about somebody being a "winner" and somebody being a "loser." What you want to be is a battler. They are the ones that win the great majority of the time. It's been said that rarely are boxers truly knocked out in fights. They just choose not to get up. As Winston Churchill said, "If you are going through hell, keep going!" The fire within you is big enough to roast any challenge dumb enough to mess with you. And how often do we make some challenges out to be bigger than what they truly are?

I was leading a group motivational tour to Charleston, S.C. one time. Our motor coach driver wheeled us down what I thought was an extremely narrow street. He had hopes that he could turn left at the end of it. There were cars parked on both sides of us. My initial interpretation was that those cars were "just inches away from us." We got to the end of the road and there was no way to turn left our right.

"That's it," I thought. "We're cooked. They're going to have to fly in a massive helicopter and lift our motor coach out."

Gary the motor coach driver didn't flinch. He knew better. He suggested the tour host Sherrill Lee and I get out to help him go backwards. I was like, "Oh, great." We got off and I was startled to see reality. The cars were actually four or five feet away on each side. The motor coach started going "Beep Beep Beep" as Gary steadily backed out. He really didn't need our help.

I got back on and shook my head. What I thought was inches on both sides and terrible trouble turned out to be not so bad after all.

Stokers don't let age dictate what they do in their lives. They go by the 60/100 formula. My grandfather, Everett Adams, who I wrote about earlier in this chapter, lived to be over 100 productive years. He may have retired from Education, but he didn't retire from life. He worked his vegetable garden and his rose garden well into his 90's. Granpapa and his wife traveled all over to see their grandchildren. They were active physically and mentally. Because of him, we can look at life this way. You expect to live to be 100. You generally start adulthood at 20. Therefore, when you get to be 60, you are halfway through adulthood. You are looking at 40 more years to do all kinds of things! When you are 80, you are halfway through the second half of your life. Forget this "start the Golden Years at age 65" nonsense.

Dr. Robert Morris is a professor of Greek, Bible, Theology, and Pastoral Ministries at Bethel College in Mishawaka, Indiana. After hearing the

Stoke the Fire Within keynote, he came up to me in total agreement of how to look at "age." This is a man who knows the Bible thoroughly.

"I can't find anything about retirement anywhere in the Bible," he said. "I don't know how to spell the word myself!"

I laughed.

"I'm 77 and going as strong as ever," he said. "I feel better than I did 20 years ago!"

There you go!

"Seniors" can be inspirations to the younger generations. Treva Hoffman was born in 1912. Well into her 90's she still goes to the Sunday service at St. John United Church of Christ in tiny Wyatt, Indiana. She lives alone. She has a prosthetic leg. Those things don't stop Treva. She's always in her pew.

I spoke at her church one time. Afterwards I was talking with one of their members, Brian Schlarb. He went on and on about how Treva was an inspiration to the "younger" folks at the church. "It can be the dead of February with snow and bitter cold weather outside," Brian said, "and you wake up and say 'it would be good to stay indoors.' But, you know that Treva will be at church, and if Treva can make it, so can the rest of us. She's a reason so many of us makes it every Sunday."

Stokers "get it" when it comes to realizing that every day is a blessing. Instead of "Oh, no, it's Monday," they go "Yes! It's Monday!" As the late Cubs broadcaster Harry Caray said, "Suck the marrow out of the bone of life!" Now, in Harry's case that often meant late nights on Rush Street in Chicago. That's not necessarily how we should view life, but it does hit home as far as getting everything out of it! Harry knew about the Art of Living. He soaked up every day! The Pointer Sisters used to have a hit song entitled "Let's Get Excited." That's how Stokers approach life. They are like a mosquito at a nudist camp. Excited! Think about how fired up a mosquito would be who was cruising through the woods and suddenly came upon a nudist camp. He'd be going, "Oh, yeah. Yeah! No long sleeves or Off repellant to deal with here!" That's how excited we can strive to be every day!

Well, as they say in the Kentucky Derby, it's "down the stretch they come" for this book. It is my hope that these Peak Performance insights have helped to enhance your life. I wanted to conclude with these summarizing thoughts.

There is one thing you must always remember.

You might want to write this down on an index card and emblaze it into your mind and heart. It is this: YOU are capable AND worthy of succeeding!

Think about that for a minute, and brand it into you like a cowboy branding young cattle.

The Optimist Club is a wonderful service organization. I remember being at one of their weekly gatherings to see how they could serve their particular community. They started off by reciting the ten points of their Optimist Creed, which was written by Christian D. Larsen. One of the lines was this: "To think of only the best, to work for only the best, and to expect only the best." I made a commitment to put that one to memory, and I often recite it in my head and heart.

I encourage you to think of that gruff camera man every time you make a decision in life. Are you going to "run the steps" like he made me that night in Philadelphia, or are you going to do it the basic tripod way?

Care deeply like that preacher man that roared into the movie theatre lobby saying, "Someone has got to stop this!"

Leave your blood in the bricks of wherever your work, live and worship.

Challenges will come at you, like those go karts

came at me, but they are never in control. Be as committed as I was to staying in the inside lane in that silly go kart!

C + D = E. Commitment plus Determination equals (and leads to) Excellence.

Be as determined as Brett Eastburn, but don't jump on your boss to get a promotion like he did!

Set short term goals like the wrestler Nick Missos, who at first simply wanted to make it a minute before getting pinned.

Seek excellence like Darin Pritchet, the radio broadcaster who never says "uh."

Separate yourself like Elaine Hessell, the girl who had her Dad throw the basketball off the uneven grain bin.

Make a formal decision to excel.

Determine where you need to say "No More" in your life.

Don't just say "I love you." Show it.

Poke fun at yourself like Mike Edwards did with his artificial leg.

Take Sandra Herron's perspective of life: "You can celebrate life or suffer it, and it has absolutely nothing to do with your circumstances."

Put the right kind of Initial Spin on every encounter.

TV newscasts come on when they're supposed to every single time, every single day. You can too.

Be a Solution Freak. Cut back on the "they should's."

Encourage. This world has never needed it more.

And, always remember that you have a fire within you! When it is stoked, you are unstoppable!

ABOUT THE AUTHOR

Charlie Adams is a successful author, professional speaker, corporate trainer and personal success coach who is an authority on kindling the flames of excellence within people and helping them ignite to success.

His engaging, entertaining and motivating keynotes and workshops have been captivating audiences for two decades. Company leaders call on Charlie to bring his invigorating message to help grow their people in such areas as personal excellence, team building, leadership and customer service.

Charlie hosts several group inspirational/humor trips a year for Edgerton's Travel Service of the northern Indiana/Chicago area. Charlie shares wit and wisdom as travelers go to such locations as Alaska, Hawaii, California Wine Country, Charleston/Savannah, Italy, Branson, Williamsburg before Christmas, and the Colorado Rockies by Train. For brochures and detailed information on "Travels

with Charlie" contact Edgerton's Travel Service at
1 800 643 4604

Charlie was an award winning broadcast journalist
in such locations as New Orleans, Memphis, south
ern California, and South Bend. As a TV News
and Sports anchor and reporter, Charlie focused
on positive news coverage. He interviewed over
1500 high achievers in his 23 years of broadcasting
across America.

Charlie and his wife Nancy and their children
make their home in Mishawaka, IN near the University of Notre Dame.

To bring Charlie to your next event you can contact his office at StokeTheFireWithin.com